Non-League Football Supporters' Guide & Yearbook 2016

EDITOR
John Robinson

Twenty-fourth Edition

For details of our range of 2,000 books and over 350 DVDs, visit our web site or contact us using the information shown below.

British Library Cataloguing in Publication Data
A catalogue record for this book is available from the British Library

ISBN: 978-1-86223-316-4

Copyright © 2015, SOCCER BOOKS LIMITED (01472 696226)
72 St. Peter's Avenue, Cleethorpes, N.E. Lincolnshire, DN35 8HU, England

Web site www.soccer-books.co.uk • e-mail info@soccer-books.co.uk

All rights are reserved. No part of this publication may be reproduced, stored in a retrieval system or transmitted, in any form or by any means, electronic, mechanical, photocopying, recording, or otherwise, without the prior written permission of Soccer Books Limited.

The Publishers, and the Football Clubs itemised are unable to accept liability for any loss, damage or injury caused by error or inaccuracy in the information published in this guide.

Manufactured in the UK by Ashford Colour Press Ltd.

FOREWORD

Our thanks go to the numerous club officials who have aided us in the compilation of information contained in this guide as well as Michael Robinson (page layouts), Bob Budd (cover artwork) and Tony Brown (Cup Statistics – www.soccerdata.com).

Any readers who have up-to-date ground photographs which they would like us to consider for use in a future edition of this guide are requested to contact us at our address which is shown on the facing page.

The fixtures listed later in this book were released just a short time before we went to print and, as such, some of the dates shown may be subject to change. We therefore suggest that readers treat these fixtures as a rough guide and check dates carefully before attending matches.

We would like to wish our readers a safe and happy spectating season.

John Robinson
EDITOR

CONTENTS

The Vanarama National League Clubs & Information 5-29
The Vanarama National League North Clubs & Information 30-52
The Vanarama National League South Clubs & Information 53-75
2014/2015 Statistics for the Football Conference National 76
2014/2015 Statistics for the Football Conference North 77
2014/2015 Statistics for the Football Conference South 78
2014/2015 Statistics for the Evo-Stik Northern League Premier Division 79
2014/2015 Statistics for the Evo-Stik Southern League – Premier Division .. 80
2014/2015 Statistics for the Ryman Football League Premier Division 81
2014/2015 F.A. Trophy Results 82-86
2014/2015 F.A. Vase Results 87-91
2015/2016 Season Fixtures for the Vanarama National League 92-94
Advertisement: The Non-League Club Directory 2016 95
Advertisement: The Supporters' Guide Series 96

THE VANARAMA NATIONAL LEAGUE

Address   4th Floor, 20 Waterloo Street, Birmingham   B2 5TB

Phone (0121) 643-3143

Web site   www.footballconference.co.uk

Clubs for the 2015/2016 Season

Aldershot Town FC	Page 6
Altrincham FC	Page 7
Barrow FC	Page 8
Boreham Wood FC	Page 9
Braintree Town FC	Page 10
Bromley FC	Page 11
Cheltenham Town FC	Page 12
Chester FC	Page 13
Dover Athletic FC	Page 14
Eastleigh FC	Page 15
FC Halifax Town	Page 16
Forest Green Rovers FC	Page 17
Gateshead FC	Page 18
Grimsby Town FC	Page 19
Guiseley FC	Page 20
Kidderminster Harriers FC	Page 21
Lincoln City FC	Page 22
Macclesfield Town	Page 23
Southport FC	Page 24
Torquay United FC	Page 25
Tranmere Rovers FC	Page 26
Welling United FC	Page 27
Woking FC	Page 28
Wrexham FC	Page 29

ALDERSHOT TOWN FC

Founded: 2013 (as a new company)
Former Names: Aldershot Town FC
Nickname: 'Shots'
Ground: Recreation Ground, High Street, Aldershot, GU11 1TW
Record Attendance: 7,500 (18th November 2000)
Pitch Size: 117 × 76 yards

Colours: Red shirts with Blue shorts
Telephone Nº: (01252) 320211
Fax Number: (01252) 324347
Club Secretary: (01252) 320211 – Bob Green
Ground Capacity: 6,500
Seating Capacity: 1,879
Web site: www.theshots.co.uk
E-mail: enquiries@theshots.co.uk

GENERAL INFORMATION
Supporters Club: c/o Club
Telephone Nº: (01252) 320211
Car Parking: Parsons Barracks Car Park is adjacent
Coach Parking: Contact the club for information
Nearest Railway Station: Aldershot (5 mins. walk)
Nearest Bus Station: Aldershot (5 minutes walk)
Club Shop: At the ground
Opening Times: Saturday matchdays 10.00am to 2.45pm and 9.30am to 7.30pm on Tuesday matchdays.
Telephone Nº: (01252) 320211

GROUND INFORMATION
Away Supporters' Entrances & Sections:
Accommodation in the East Bank Terrace, Bill Warren section (South Stand) – Redan Hill Turnstiles Nº 11 and 12.

ADMISSION INFO (2015/2016 PRICES)
Adult Standing: £17.00
Adult Seating: £19.00
Ages 11 to 16 Standing: £5.00
Ages 11 to 16 Seating: £7.00
Note: Under-11s are admitted free with paying adults – a maximum of 2 children per adult.
Concessionary Standing: £13.00
Concessionary Seating: £15.00
Note: Military personnel are charged Concessionary prices
Programme Price: £3.00

DISABLED INFORMATION
Wheelchairs: Accommodated in the North Stand
Helpers: Admitted
Prices: £13.00 for the disabled, free of charge for helpers
Disabled Toilets: Available
Contact: (01252) 320211 (Bookings are required)

Travelling Supporters' Information:
Routes: From the M3: Exit at Junction 4 and follow signs for Aldershot (A331). Leave the A331 at the A323 exit (Ash Road) and continue along into the High Street. The ground is just past the Railway Bridge on the right; From the A31: Continue along the A31 to the junction with the A331, then as above; From the A325 (Farnborough Road): Follow signs to the A323 then turn left into Wellington Avenue. The ground is just off the 2nd roundabout on the left – the floodlights are clearly visible.

ALTRINCHAM FC

Founded: 1891
Former Names: Broadheath FC
Nickname: 'The Robins'
Ground: The J. Davidson Stadium, Moss Lane, Altrincham WA15 8AP
Record Attendance: 10,275 (February 1925)
Pitch Size: 110 × 72 yards
Web site: www.altrinchamfc.com

Colours: Red and White striped shirts, Black shorts
Telephone Nº: (0161) 928-1045
Daytime Phone Nº: (0161) 928-1045
Fax Number: (0161) 926-9934
Ground Capacity: 6,085
Seating Capacity: 1,154
E-mail: office@altrinchamfootballclub.co.uk

GENERAL INFORMATION
Car Parking: Limited street parking
Coach Parking: By Police Direction
Nearest Railway Station: Altrincham (15 minutes walk)
Nearest Bus Station: Altrincham
Club Shop: Inside the ground
Opening Times: Matchdays only. Opens one hour prior to the start of the game.
Telephone Nº: (0161) 928-1045

GROUND INFORMATION
Away Supporters' Entrances & Sections:
Hale End turnstiles and accommodation

ADMISSION INFO (2015/2016 PRICES)
Adult Standing: £14.00
Adult Seating: £15.00
Concessionary Standing: £9.00
Concessionary Seating: £10.00
Ages 12-16 years Standing/Seating: £5.00
Under-12s Standing/Seating: £2.00

DISABLED INFORMATION
Wheelchairs: 3 spaces are available each for home and away fans adjacent to the Away dugout
Helpers: Admitted
Prices: £14.00 combined price for a disabled fan and helper
Disabled Toilets: Yes
Contact: (0161) 928-1045 (Bookings are necessary)

Travelling Supporters' Information:
Routes: Exit the M56 at either Junction 6 or 7 and follow the signs for Altrincham FC.

BARROW FC

Founded: 1901
Former Names: None
Nickname: 'Bluebirds'
Ground: Furness Building Society Stadium, Barrow-in-Furness, Cumbria   LA14 5UW
Record Attendance: 16,874 (1954)
Pitch Size: 110 × 75 yards

Colours: White shirts with Blue shorts
Telephone Nº: (01229) 823061
Fax Number: (01229) 823061
Ground Capacity: 4,057
Seating Capacity: 928
Web site: www.barrowafc.com
E-mail: office@barrowafc.com

GENERAL INFORMATION
Car Parking: Street Parking, Popular Side Car Park and Soccer Bar Car Park
Coach Parking: Adjacent to the ground
Nearest Railway Station: Barrow Central (½ mile)
Nearest Bus Station: ½ mile
Club Shop: At the ground
Opening Times: Monday to Friday 9.00am – 3.30pm and Saturdays 10.00am – 2.00pm
Telephone Nº: (01229) 823061

GROUND INFORMATION
Away Supporters' Entrances & Sections:
West Terrace (not covered)

ADMISSION INFO   (2015/2016 PRICES)
Adult Standing: £14.00
Adult Seating: £15.00
Concessionary Standing: £11.00
Concessionary Seating: £12.00
Ages 11 to 17 Standing/Seating: £5.00
Under-11s Standing/Seating: £1.00

DISABLED INFORMATION
Wheelchairs: 6 spaces available in the Disabled Area
Helpers: Admitted
Prices: Normal prices apply
Disabled Toilets: Available
Contact: (01229) 823061   (Bookings are not necessary)

Travelling Supporters' Information:
Routes: Exit the M6 at Junction 36 and take the A590 through Ulverston. Using the bypass, follow signs for Barrow. After approximately 5 miles, turn left into Wilkie Road and the ground is on the right.

BOREHAM WOOD FC

Founded: 1948
Former Names: Boreham Rovers FC and Royal Retournez FC
Nickname: 'The Wood'
Ground: Meadow Park, Broughinge Road, Borehamwood, Hertfordshire WD6 5AL
Record Attendance: 4,030 (2002)
Pitch Size: 112 × 72 yards

Colours: White shirts with Black shorts
Telephone N°: (0208) 953-5097
Fax Number: (0208) 207-7982
Ground Capacity: 3,960
Seating Capacity: 1,401
Web site: www.borehamwoodfootballclub.co.uk

GENERAL INFORMATION
Car Parking: At the ground or in Brook Road car park
Coach Parking: At the ground
Nearest Railway Station: Elstree & Borehamwood (1 mile)
Nearest Bus Station: Barnet
Club Shop: At the ground
Opening Times: 11.00am to 10.00pm Monday to Thursday; 11.00am to 6.00pm at weekends
Telephone N°: (0208) 953-5097

GROUND INFORMATION
Away Supporters' Entrances & Sections:
No usual segregation

ADMISSION INFO (2015/2016 PRICES)
Adult Standing: £16.00
Adult Seating: £16.00
Under-16s Standing/Seating: £8.50
Senior Citizen Standing/Seating: £10.00

DISABLED INFORMATION
Wheelchairs: Accommodated
Helpers: Admitted
Prices: Concessionary prices are charged for the disabled and helpers
Disabled Toilets: Available
Contact: (0208) 953-5097 (Bookings are necessary)

Travelling Supporters' Information:
Routes: Exit the M25 at Junction 23 and take the A1 South. After 2 miles, take the Borehamwood exit onto the dual carriageway and go over the flyover following signs for Borehamwood for 1 mile. Turn right at the Studio roundabout into Brook Road, then next right into Broughinge Road for the ground.

BRAINTREE TOWN FC

Founded: 1898
Former Names: Manor Works FC, Crittall Athletic FC, Braintree & Crittall Athletic FC and Braintree FC
Nickname: 'The Iron'
Ground: Amlin Stadium, Clockhouse Way, Braintree, Essex   CM7 3RD
Record Attendance: 4,000 (May 1952)
Pitch Size: 111 × 78 yards
Ground Capacity: 4,222
Seating Capacity: 553

Colours: Orange shirts and socks with Blue shorts
Telephone Nº: (01376) 345617
Fax Number: (01376) 330976
Correspondence Address: Tom Woodley, 19A Bailey Bridge Road, Braintree   CM7 5TT
Contact Telephone Nº: (01376) 326234
Web site: www.braintreetownfc.org.uk
E-mail: braintreetfc@aol.com

GENERAL INFORMATION
Car Parking: At the ground
Coach Parking: At the ground
Nearest Railway Station: Braintree (1 mile)
Nearest Bus Station: Braintree
Club Shop: At the ground
Opening Times: Matchdays only
Telephone Nº: (01376) 345617

GROUND INFORMATION
Away Supporters' Entrances & Sections: Gates 7-8

ADMISSION INFO (2015/2016 PRICES)
Adult Standing: £16.00 – £18.00
Adult Seating: £16.00 – £18.00
Concessionary Standing: £11.00
Concessionary Seating: £12.00
Under-16s Standing: £6.00
Under-11s Standing: £4.00
Note: Prices vary depending on the category of the game

DISABLED INFORMATION
Wheelchairs: Accommodated – 6 spaces available in the Main Stand
Helpers: Admitted
Prices: Normal prices apply
Disabled Toilets: Available
Contact: (01376) 345617

Travelling Supporters' Information:
Routes: Exit the A120 Braintree Bypass at the McDonald's roundabout and follow Cressing Road northwards. The floodlights at the ground are visible on the left ½ mile into town. Turn left into Clockhouse Way then left again for the ground.

BROMLEY FC

Founded: 1892
Former Names: None
Nickname: 'Lillywhites'
Ground: The Stadium, Hayes Lane, Bromley, Kent, BR2 9EF
Record Attendance: 12,000 (24th September 1949)
Pitch Size: 112 × 72 yards

Colours: White shirts with Black shorts
Telephone Nº: (020) 8460-5291
Fax Number: (020) 8313-3992
Ground Capacity: 3,300
Seating Capacity: 1,300
Web site: www.bromleyfc.net
E-mail: info@bromleyfc.net

GENERAL INFORMATION
Car Parking: 300 spaces available at the ground
Coach Parking: At the ground
Nearest Railway Station: Bromley South (1 mile)
Nearest Bus Station: High Street, Bromley
Club Shop: At the ground
Opening Times: Matchdays only
Telephone Nº: (020) 8460-5291

GROUND INFORMATION
Away Supporters' Entrances & Sections:
No usual segregation

ADMISSION INFO (2015/2016 PRICES)
Adult Standing/Seating: £15.00
Concessionary Standing/Seating: £10.00
Under-16s/Student Standing/Seating: £5.00
Note: Under-16s are admitted free of charge with a paying adult for advance purchases up to 1 hour before kick-off. A special £10.00 discounted price is available for Season Ticket holders of Premiership and Football League clubs.

DISABLED INFORMATION
Wheelchairs: Accommodated
Helpers: Admitted
Prices: Please phone the club for information
Disabled Toilets: Yes
Contact: (0181) 460-5291 (Bookings are necessary)

Travelling Supporters' Information:
Routes: Exit the M25 at Junction 4 and follow the A21 for Bromley and London for approximately 4 miles before forking left onto the A232 signposted for Croydon/Sutton. At the second set of traffic lights turn right into Baston Road (B265) and follow for approximately 2 miles as it becomes Hayes Street and then Hayes Lane. The ground is on the right just after a mini-roundabout.

CHELTENHAM TOWN FC

Founded: 1887
Nickname: 'Robins'
Ground: Abbey Business Stadium, Whaddon Road, Cheltenham, Gloucestershire GL52 5NA
Ground Capacity: 7,136
Seating Capacity: 4,054
Record Attendance: 8,326 (1956)

Pitch Size: 110 × 72 yards
Colours: Red and White striped shirts, Black shorts
Telephone Nº: (01242) 573558
Fax Number: (01242) 224675
Web Site: www.ctfc.com
E-mail: info@ctfc.com

GENERAL INFORMATION
Car Parking: Available at the ground for a £5.00 charge
Coach Parking: Please phone for details
Nearest Railway Station: Cheltenham Spa (2½ miles)
Nearest Bus Station: Cheltenham Royal Well
Club Shop: At the ground
Opening Times: Weekdays & Matchdays 10.00am–2.45pm
Telephone Nº: (01242) 573558

GROUND INFORMATION
Away Supporters' Entrances & Sections:
Hazlewoods Stand (entrance from Whaddon Road) or the In2Print Stand

ADMISSION INFO (2015/2016 PRICES)
Adult Standing: £16.00
Adult Seating: £20.00 or £21.00
Under-18s Standing: £5.00
Under-18s Seating: £7.00
Concessionary Standing: £12.00
Concessionary Seating: £14.00 – £15.00
Programme Price: £3.00

DISABLED INFORMATION
Wheelchairs: Accommodated in front of the Main Stand (use main entrance) and in the In 2 Print Stand
Helpers: Admitted free of charge
Prices: Concessionary prices are charged
Disabled Toilets: Available in the In 2 Print Stand, adjacent to the Stagecoach West Stand and in the Social Club
Contact: (01242) 573558 (Bookings are necessary)

Travelling Supporters' Information:
Routes: The ground is situated to the North-East of Cheltenham, 1 mile from the Town Centre off the B4632 (Prestbury Road) – Whaddon Road is to the East of the B4632 just North of Pittville Circus. Road signs in the vicinity indicate 'Whaddon Road/Cheltenham Town FC'.

CHESTER FC

Founded: 1885
Former Names: Chester FC and Chester City FC
Nickname: 'City'
Ground: Swansway Chester Stadium, Bumpers Lane, Chester CH1 4LT
Pitch Size: 116 × 75 yards
Record Attendance: 5,987 (17th April 2004)

Colours: Blue and White striped shirts, Black shorts
Ground Telephone N°: (01244) 371376
Ticket Office: (01244) 371376
Fax Number: (01244) 390265
Ground Capacity: 5,400
Seating Capacity: 4,170
Web site: www.chesterfc.com
E-mail: info@chesterfc.com

GENERAL INFORMATION

Car Parking: Ample spaces available at the ground (£1.00)
Coach Parking: Available at the ground
Nearest Railway Station: Chester (2 miles)
Nearest Bus Station: Chester (1½ miles)
Club Shop: At the ground
Opening Times: Weekdays & matchdays 10.00am–4.00pm
Telephone N°: (01244) 371376

GROUND INFORMATION

Away Supporters' Entrances & Sections:
South Stand for covered seating and also part of the West Stand

ADMISSION INFO (2015/2016 PRICES)

Adult Standing: £15.00   **Adult Seating**: £18.00
Senior Citizen Standing: £10.00
Senior Citizen Seating: £12.00
Under-21s Seating/Standing: £10.00
Ages 16 and 17 Seating/Standing: £5.00
Under-16s Seating/Standing: £3.00 (Under-5s free)

DISABLED INFORMATION

Wheelchairs: 32 spaces for wheelchairs (with 40 helpers) in the West Stand and East Stand
Helpers: One helper admitted per disabled person
Prices: Concessionary prices for the disabled. Free for helpers
Disabled Toilets: Available in West and East Stands
Contact: (01244) 371376 (Bookings are necessary)

Travelling Supporters' Information:
Routes: From the North: Take the M56, A41 or A56 into the Town Centre and then follow Queensferry (A548) signs into Sealand Road. Turn left at the traffic lights by 'Tesco' into Bumpers Lane – the ground is ½ mile at the end of the road; From the East: Take the A54 or A51 into the Town Centre (then as North); From the South: Take the A41 or A483 into Town Centre (then as North); From the West: Take the A55, A494 or A548 and follow Queensferry signs towards Birkenhead (A494) and after 1¼ miles bear left onto the A548 (then as North); From the M6/M56 (Avoiding Town Centre): Take the M56 to Junction 16 (signposted Queensferry), turn left at the roundabout onto A5117, signposted Wales. At the next roundabout turn left onto the A5480 (signposted Chester) and after approximately 3 miles take the 3rd exit from the roundabout (signposted Sealand Road Industrial Parks). Go straight across 2 sets of traffic lights into Bumpers Lane. The ground is ½ mile on the right.

DOVER ATHLETIC FC

Founded: 1983
Former Names: None
Nickname: 'The Whites'
Ground: Crabble Athletic Ground, Lewisham Road, River, Dover CT17 0JB
Record Attendance: 4,186 (2002)
Pitch Size: 111 × 73 yards

Colours: White shirts with Black shorts
Telephone Nº: (01304) 822373
Fax Number: (01304) 821383
Ground Capacity: 6,500
Seating Capacity: 1,000
Web site: www.doverathletic.com
E-mail: enquiries@doverathletic.com

GENERAL INFORMATION
Car Parking: Street parking
Coach Parking: Street parking
Nearest Railway Station: Kearsney (1 mile)
Nearest Bus Station: Pencester Road, Dover (1½ miles)
Club Shop: At the ground
Opening Times: Saturdays 9.00am to 12.00pm
Telephone Nº: (01304) 822373

GROUND INFORMATION
Away Supporters' Entrances & Sections: Segregation only used when required

ADMISSION INFO (2015/2016 PRICES)
Adult Standing: £15.00
Adult Seating: £16.50
Senior Citizen Standing: £12.00
Senior Citizen Seating: £14.00
Under-18s Standing: £6.00
Under-18s Seating: £7.50
Under-11s Standing/Seating: Free of charge

DISABLED INFORMATION
Wheelchairs: Approximately 20 spaces are available in front of the Family Stand
Helpers: Please phone the club for information
Prices: Please phone the club for information
Disabled Toilets: None
Contact: – (Bookings are not necessary)

Travelling Supporters' Information:
Routes: Take the A2 to the Whitfield roundabout and take the 4th exit. Travel down the hill to the mini-roundabout then turn left and follow the road for 1 mile to the traffic lights on the hill. Turn sharp right and pass under the railway bridge – the ground is on the left after 300 yards.

EASTLEIGH FC

Founded: 1946
Former Names: Swaythling Athletic FC and Swaythling FC
Nickname: 'The Spitfires'
Ground: The Silverlake Stadium, Stoneham Lane, Eastleigh SO50 9HT
Record Attendance: 3,104 (2006)
Pitch Size: 112 × 74 yards

Colours: Blue shirts with White shorts
Telephone Nº: (023) 8061-3361
Fax Number: (023) 8061-2379
Ground Capacity: 6,000
Seating Capacity: 2,812
Web site: www.eastleighfc.com
e-mail: admin@eastleighfc.com

GENERAL INFORMATION
Car Parking: Spaces for 450 cars available (hard standing)
Coach Parking: At the ground
Nearest Railway Station: Southampton Parkway (¾ mile)
Nearest Bus Station: Eastleigh (2 miles)
Club Shop: At the ground
Opening Times: Matchdays and during functions only

GROUND INFORMATION
Away Supporters' Entrances & Sections:
Segregation in force for some games only. Please contact the club for further details

ADMISSION INFO (2015/2016 PRICES)
Adult Standing: £12.00
Adult Seating: £15.00
Concessionary Standing: £7.50
Concessionary Seating: £10.00
Under-16s Standing/Seating: £4.00 or £5.00
Under-7s Standing/Seating: Free of charge

DISABLED INFORMATION
Wheelchairs: Accommodated
Helpers: Admitted
Prices: Concessionary prices apply
Disabled Toilets: Available
Contact: (023) 8061-3361 (Bookings are not necessary)

Travelling Supporters' Information:
Routes: Exit the M27 at Junction 5 (signposted for Southampton Airport) and take the A335 (Stoneham Way) towards Southampton. After ½ mile, turn right at the traffic lights into Bassett Green Road. Turn right at the next set of traffic lights into Stoneham Lane and the ground is on the right after ¾ mile.

FC HALIFAX TOWN

Founded: 1911 (Re-formed 2008)
Former Names: Halifax Town FC
Nickname: 'The Shaymen'
Ground: The Shay Stadium, Shay Syke, Halifax, HX1 2YT
Ground Capacity: 10,568
Seating Capacity: 5,285

Record Attendance: 4,023 (1st January 2011)
Pitch Size: 112 × 73 yards
Colours: Blue shirts and shorts
Telephone Nº: (01422) 341222
Fax Number: (01422) 349487
Web Site: www.fcht.co.uk

GENERAL INFORMATION

Car Parking: Adjacent to the East Stand and also Shaw Hill Car Park (Nearby)
Coach Parking: By arrangement with the Club Secretary
Nearest Railway Station: Halifax (10 minutes walk)
Nearest Bus Station: Halifax (15 minutes walk)
Club Shop: At the ground in the East Stand
Opening Times: Please phone for details
Telephone Nº: (01422) 341222 (to change during the 2011/12 season)

GROUND INFORMATION

Away Supporters' Entrances & Sections:
Skircoat Stand (Seating only)

ADMISSION INFO (2015/2016 PRICES)

Adult Standing/Seating: £17.00
Under-16s Standing/Seating: £6.00
Senior Citizen Standing/Seating: £13.00
Under-12s Standing/Seating: £6.00
Under-7s Standing/Seating: £3.00

DISABLED INFORMATION

Wheelchairs: 33 spaces available in total in disabled sections in the East Stand and South Stand
Helpers: One admitted free with each paying disabled fan
Prices: Free of charge for the disabled and helpers
Disabled Toilets: Available in the East and South Stands
Contact: (01422) 434212 (Bookings are not necessary)

Travelling Supporters' Information:
Routes: From the North: Take the A629 to Halifax Town Centre. Take the 2nd exit at the roundabout into Broad Street and follow signs for Huddersfield (A629) into Skircoat Road; From the South, East and West: Exit the M62 at Junction 24 and follow Halifax (A629) signs for the Town Centre into Skircoat Road then Shaw Hill for ground.

FOREST GREEN ROVERS FC

Founded: 1889
Former Names: Stroud FC
Nickname: 'The Green Devils'
Ground: The New Lawn, Another Way, Forest Green, Nailsworth, Gloucestershire, GL6 0FG
Record Attendance: 4,836 (3rd January 2009)
Pitch Size: 110 × 70 yards

Colours: Black and White striped shirts, Black shorts
Telephone N°: (01453) 834860
Fax Number: (01453) 835291
Ground Capacity: 5,025
Seating Capacity: 1,881
Web site: www.forestgreenroversfc.com
E-mail: reception@forestgreenroversfc.com

GENERAL INFORMATION
Car Parking: At the ground
Coach Parking: At the ground
Nearest Railway Station: Stroud (4 miles)
Nearest Bus Station: Nailsworth
Club Shop: At the ground
Opening Times: Monday to Friday 9.00am to 3.00pm
Telephone N°: (01453) 834860

GROUND INFORMATION
Away Supporters' Entrances & Sections:
EESI Stand

ADMISSION INFO (2015/2016 PRICES)
Adult Standing: £15.00   **Adult Seating**: £17.00–£19.00
Senior Citizen Standing: £11.00
Senior Citizen Seating: £13.00 – £15.00
Child Standing: £4.00   **Child Seating**: £6.00 – £7.00
Young Adult Standing: £7.00
Young Adult Seating: £9.00 – £11.00

DISABLED INFORMATION
Wheelchairs: Accommodated in the Main Stand
Helpers: Admitted
Prices: Normal prices for the disabled. Free for helpers
Disabled Toilets: Yes
Contact: (01453) 834860   (Enquiries necessary at least 72 hours in advance)

Travelling Supporters' Information:
Routes: The ground is located 4 miles south of Stroud on the A46 to Bath. Upon entering Nailsworth, turn into Spring Hill at the mini-roundabout and the ground is approximately ½ mile up the hill on the left.

GATESHEAD FC

Founded: 1930 (Reformed in 1977)
Former Names: Gateshead United FC
Nickname: 'Tynesiders'
Ground: International Stadium, Neilson Road, Gateshead NE10 0EF
Record Attendance: 11,750 (1995)
Pitch Size: 110 × 70 yards

Colours: White shirts with Black shorts
Telephone Nº: (0191) 478-3883
Fax Number: (0191) 440-0404
Ground Capacity: 11,750
Seating Capacity: 11,750
Web site: www.gateshead-fc.com
E-mail: info@gateshead-fc.com

GENERAL INFORMATION
Car Parking: At the stadium
Coach Parking: At the stadium
Nearest Railway Station: Gateshead Stadium Metro (½ mile); Newcastle (British Rail) 1½ miles
Nearest Bus Station: Heworth Interchange (½ mile)
Club Shop: At the stadium
Opening Times: Matchdays only
Telephone Nº: (0191) 478-3883

GROUND INFORMATION
Away Supporters' Entrances & Sections:
Tyne & Wear County Stand North End or the East Stand

ADMISSION INFO (2015/2016 PRICES)
Adult Seating: £15.00
Senior Citizen/Concessionary Seating: £10.00
Under-16s Seating: £3.00
Under-18s/Student Seating: £8.00
Note: Tickets are cheaper when purchased in advance.

DISABLED INFORMATION
Wheelchairs: 5 spaces available each for home and away fans by the trackside – Level access with automatic doors
Helpers: Admitted
Prices: Normal prices for the disabled. Helpers are admitted free of charge.
Disabled Toilets: Available in the Reception Area and on the 1st floor concourse – accessible by lift.
Contact: (0191) 478-3883 (Bookings are necessary)

Travelling Supporters' Information:
Routes: From the South: Take the A1(M) to Washington Services and fork right onto the A194(M) signposted Tyne Tunnel. At the next roundabout, turn left onto the A184 signposted for Gateshead. The Stadium is on the right after 3 miles.

GRIMSBY TOWN FC

Founded: 1878
Former Names: Grimsby Pelham FC (1879)
Nickname: 'Mariners'
Ground: Blundell Park, Cleethorpes DN35 7PY
Ground Capacity: 8,974 (All seats)
Record Attendance: 31,651 (20th February 1937)
Pitch Size: 111 × 74 yards

Colours: Black and White striped shirts, Black shorts
Telephone Nº: (01472) 605050
Ticket Office: (01472) 605050 (Option 4)
Fax Number: (01472) 693665
Web Site: www.grimsby-townfc.co.uk
E-mail: info@gtfc.co.uk

GENERAL INFORMATION
Car Parking: Street parking
Coach Parking: Harrington Street – near the ground
Nearest Railway Station: Cleethorpes (1½ miles)
Nearest Bus Station: Brighowgate, Grimsby (4 miles)
Club Shop: At the ground
Opening Times: Monday – Friday 9.00am to 5.00pm; Matchday Saturdays 9.00am to kick-off
Telephone Nº: (01472) 605050

GROUND INFORMATION
Away Supporters' Entrances & Sections:
Harrington Street turnstiles 15-18 and Constitution Avenue turnstiles 5-14

ADMISSION INFO (2015/2016 PRICES)
Adult Seating: £18.00 (Away fans £18.00)
Senior Citizen/Student Seating: £12.00
Young Adults Seating (Ages 15–18): £12.00
Child Seating: £4.00 – £6.00 (Under-15s)
Note: Tickets are cheaper if purchased before the matchday

DISABLED INFORMATION
Wheelchairs: 50 spaces in total for Home and Away fans in the disabled section, in front of the Main Stand
Helpers: Helpers are admitted
Prices: £18.00 for the disabled. Free of charge for helpers
Disabled Toilets: Available in disabled section
Commentaries are available in disabled section
Contact: (01472) 605050 (Bookings are necessary)

Travelling Supporters' Information:
Routes: From All Parts except Lincolnshire and East Anglia: Take the M180 to the A180 and follow signs for Grimsby/Cleethorpes. The A180 ends at a roundabout (the 3rd in short distance after crossing docks), take the 2nd exit from the roundabout over the Railway flyover into Cleethorpes Road (A1098) and continue into Grimsby Road. After the second stretch of dual carriageway, the ground is ½ mile on the left; From Lincolnshire: Take the A46 or A16 and follow Cleethorpes signs along (A1098) Weelsby Road for 2 miles. Take the 1st exit at the roundabout at the end of Clee Road into Grimsby Road. The ground is 1¾ miles on the right.

GUISELEY AFC

Founded: 1909
Former Names: None
Nickname: 'The Lions'
Ground: Nethermoor Park, Otley Road, Guiseley, Leeds LS20 8BT
Record Attendance: 2,486 (1989/90)
Pitch Size: 110 × 69 yards

Colours: White shirts with Navy Blue shorts
Telephone N°: 07946 388739
Social Club Phone N°: (01943) 872872
Fax Number: (01943) 873223
Ground Capacity: 3,000
Seating Capacity: 518
Web site: www.guiseleyafc.co.uk
E-mail: admin@guiseleyafc.co.uk

GENERAL INFORMATION

Car Parking: At the ground and in Netherfield Road
Coach Parking: At the ground
Nearest Railway Station: Guiseley (5 minute walk)
Nearest Bus Station: Bus Stop outside the ground
Club Shop: At the ground
Opening Times: Matchdays only
Telephone N°: (01943) 879236 (weekdays)
Postal Sales: Yes

GROUND INFORMATION

Away Supporters' Entrances & Sections: No usual segregation

ADMISSION INFO (2015/2016 PRICES)

Adult Standing: £15.00
Adult Seating: £15.00
Ages 12 to 16 Standing/Seating: £5.00
Under-12s Standing/Seating: Free of charge when accompanied by a paying adult
Concessionary Standing/Seating: £10.00

DISABLED INFORMATION

Wheelchairs: Accommodated by the Players' Entrance
Helpers: Admitted
Prices: Free for both disabled fans and helpers
Disabled Toilets: None
Contact: (01943) 879236 (Bookings are advisable)

Travelling Supporters' Information:
Routes: Exit the M62 at Junction 28 and take the Leeds Ring Road to the roundabout at the junction of the A65 at Horsforth. Turn left onto the A65 and pass through Rawdon to Guiseley keeping Morrison's supermarket on your left. Pass straight through the traffic lights with the Station pub or your right and the ground is on the right after ¼ mile, adjacent to the cricket field.

KIDDERMINSTER HARRIERS FC

Founded: 1886
Nickname: 'Harriers'
Ground: Aggborough, Hoo Road, Kidderminster, Worcestershire DY10 1NB
Ground Capacity: 6,444
Seating Capacity: 3,143
Record Attendance: 9,155 (1948)

Pitch Size: 110 × 72 yards
Colours: Red and White halved shirts, White shorts
Telephone Nº: (01562) 823931
Fax Number: (01562) 827329
Web Site: www.harriers.co.uk
E-mail: info@harriers.co.uk

GENERAL INFORMATION
Car Parking: At the ground
Coach Parking: As directed
Nearest Railway Station: Kidderminster
Nearest Bus Station: Kidderminster Town Centre
Club Shop: At the ground
Opening Times: Weekdays and First Team Matchdays 9.00am to 5.00pm
Telephone Nº: (01562) 823931

GROUND INFORMATION
Away Supporters' Entrances & Sections:
John Smiths Stand Entrance D and South Terrace Entrance E

ADMISSION INFO (2015/2016 PRICES)
Adult Standing: £14.00
Adult Seating: £17.00
Senior Citizen Standing: £8.00
Senior Citizen Seating: £11.00
Under-16s Standing: £5.00
Under-16s Seating: £8.00
Note: Under-5s are admitted free with a paying adult

DISABLED INFORMATION
Wheelchairs: Home fans accommodated at the front of the Main Stand, Away fans in front of the John Smiths Stand
Helpers: Admitted
Prices: £10.00 for each disabled fan plus one helper
Disabled Toilets: Available by the disabled area
Contact: (01562) 823931   (Bookings are not necessary)

Travelling Supporters' Information:
Routes: Exit the M5 at Junction 3 and follow the A456 to Kidderminster. The ground is situated close by the Severn Valley Railway Station so follow the brown Steam Train signs and turn into Hoo Road about 200 yards downhill of the station. Follow the road along for ¼ mile and the ground is on the left.

LINCOLN CITY FC

Founded: 1884
Nickname: 'Red Imps'
Ground: Sincil Bank Stadium, Lincoln LN5 8LD
Ground Capacity: 10,120 (All seats)
Record Attendance: 23,196 (15th November 1967)
Pitch Size: 110 × 72 yards

Colours: Red and White striped shirts, Black shorts
Telephone Nº: (01522) 880011
Ticket Office: (01522) 880011
Fax Number: (01522) 880020
Web Site: www.redimps.co.uk

GENERAL INFORMATION
Car Parking: Stacey West Car Park (limited parking for £5.00 per car).
Coach Parking: Please contact the club for details.
Nearest Railway Station: Lincoln Central
Club Shop: At the ground
Opening Times: Weekdays 10.00am to 2.00pm and Saturday Matchdays 10.00am until kick-off and 30 minutes after the final whistle
Telephone Nº: (01522) 880011

GROUND INFORMATION
Away Supporters' Entrances & Sections:
Lincolnshire Co-operative Stand (seated) – Turnstiles 24 & 25

ADMISSION INFO (2015/2016 PRICES)
Adult Seating: £18.00
Junior Seating: £7.00
Concessionary Seating: £13.00
Note: Discounts are available for families and for advance ticket purchases

DISABLED INFORMATION
Wheelchairs: Limited number of spaces available in the disabled section, adjacent to turnstile 23
Helpers: One helper admitted per disabled person
Prices: Applications for disabled passes must be made to the club. Wheelchair-bound disabled are charged concessionary prices. Helpers are admitted free if the disabled fan has a medium/high level disability allowance
Disabled Toilets: Adjacent to disabled area
Contact: (01522) 880011 (Bookings are necessary)

Travelling Supporters' Information:
Routes: From the East: Take the A46 or A158 into the City Centre following Newark (A46) signs into the High Street and take next left (Scorer Street and Cross Street) for the ground; From the North and West: Take the A15 or A57 into the City Centre, then as from the East; From the South: Take the A1 then A46 for the City Centre, then into the High Street, parking on the South Common or in the Stadium via South Park Avenue, turn down by the Fire Station.

MACCLESFIELD TOWN FC

Founded: 1874
Former Names: Macclesfield FC
Nickname: 'The Silkmen'
Ground: Moss Rose Ground, London Road, Macclesfield, Cheshire SK11 7SP
Ground Capacity: 5,977
Seating Capacity: 2,599
Record Attendance: 10,041 (1948)

Pitch Size: 105 × 66 yards
Colours: Blue shirts, White shorts and Blue socks
Telephone Nº: (01625) 264686
Ticket Office: (01625) 264686
Fax Number: (01625) 264692
Web Site: www.mtfc.co.uk
E-mail: office@mtfc.co.uk

GENERAL INFORMATION

Car Parking: Ample parking available near the ground
Coach Parking: Near the ground
Nearest Railway Station: Macclesfield (1 mile)
Nearest Bus Station: Macclesfield
Club Shop: At the ground
Opening Times: Weekdays and matchdays 9.00am to 5.00pm
Telephone Nº: (01625) 264686

GROUND INFORMATION

Away Supporters' Entrances & Sections:
John Askey Terrace and the left side of the Moss Lane Stand

ADMISSION INFO (2015/2016 PRICES)

Adult Standing: £15.00
Adult Seating: £19.00
Concessions Standing: £10.00
Concessions Seating: £15.00
Under-12s Standing: £3.00
Under-12s Seating: £3.00
Under-18s/Student Standing: £5.00
Under-18s/Student Seating: £5.00

DISABLED INFORMATION

Wheelchairs: 45 spaces in front of the Estate Road Stand
Helpers: One helper admitted per disabled fan
Prices: Normal prices apply for the disabled. Helpers are admitted free of charge
Disabled Toilets: 3 available
Contact: (01625) 264686 (Bookings are necessary)

Travelling Supporters' Information:
Routes: From the North: Exit the M6 at Junction 19 to Knutsford, follow the A537 to Macclesfield. Follow signs for the Town Centre, then for the A523 to Leek. The ground is 1 mile out of the Town Centre on the right; From the South: Exit the M6 at Junction 17 for Sandbach and follow the A534 to Congleton. Then take the A536 to Macclesfield. After passing The Rising Sun on the left, turn right into Moss Lane after approximately ¼ mile. Following this lane will take you to the ground.

SOUTHPORT FC

Founded: 1881
Former Names: Southport Vulcan FC, Southport Central FC
Nickname: 'The Sandgrounders' and 'The Port'
Ground: Merseyrail Community Stadium, Haig Avenue, Southport, Merseyside PR8 6JZ
Record Attendance: 20,010 (1932)
Pitch Size: 110 × 77 yards

Colours: Yellow shirts and shorts
Telephone Nº: (01704) 533422
Fax Number: (01704) 533455
Ground Capacity: 6,008
Seating Capacity: 1,660
Web site: www.southportfc.net

GENERAL INFORMATION

Car Parking: Street parking
Coach Parking: Adjacent to the ground
Nearest Railway Station: Meols Cop (½ mile)
Nearest Bus Station: Southport Town Centre
Club Shop: At the ground
Opening Times: Matchdays from 1.30pm (from 6.30pm on evening matchdays)
Telephone Nº: (01704) 533422

GROUND INFORMATION

Away Supporters' Entrances & Sections:
Blowick End entrances

ADMISSION INFO (2015/2016 PRICES)

Adult Standing: £13.50
Adult Seating: £15.00
Concessionary Standing: £10.00
Concessionary Seating: £11.00
Under-19s Standing/Seating: £5.00
Note: Children aged 11 and under are admitted free of charge when accompanied by a paying adult.

DISABLED INFORMATION

Wheelchairs: Accommodated in front of the Grandstand
Helpers: Admitted
Prices: Concessionary prices charged for the disabled. Helpers are admitted free of charge
Disabled Toilets: Available at the Blowick End of the Grandstand
Contact: (01704) 533422   (Bookings are not necessary)

Travelling Supporters' Information:
Routes: Exit the M58 at Junction 3 and take the A570 to Southport. At the major roundabout (McDonalds/Tesco) go straight on into Scarisbrick New Road, pass over the brook and turn right into Haig Avenue at the traffic lights. The ground is then on the right-hand side.

TORQUAY UNITED FC

Founded: 1899
Former Name: Torquay Town FC (1899-1910)
Nickname: 'Gulls'
Ground: Plainmoor Ground, Torquay   TQ1 3PS
Ground Capacity: 6,200   **Seating Capacity**: 2,841
Record Attendance: 21,908 (29th January 1955)
Pitch Size: 112 × 72 yards

Colours: Yellow shirts and shorts
Telephone Nº: (01803) 328666 (Option 0)
Ticket Office: (01803) 328666 (Option 0)
Fax Number: (01803) 323976
Web Site: www.torquayunited.com
E-mail: reception@torquayunited.com

GENERAL INFORMATION

Car Parking: Street parking
Coach Parking: Lymington Road Coach Station (½ mile)
Nearest Railway Station: Torquay (2 miles)
Nearest Bus Station: Lymington Road (½ mile)
Club Shop: At the ground
Opening Times: Matchdays and during Office Hours
Telephone Nº: (01803) 328666 Option 0

GROUND INFORMATION

Away Supporters' Entrances & Sections:
Babbacombe End turnstiles for Babbacombe End

ADMISSION INFO (2015/2016 PRICES)

Adult Standing: £17.00
Adult Seating: £19.00 – £21.00
Concessionary Standing: £13.00
Concessionary Seating: £15.00 – £17.00
Under-16s Standing/Seating: £6.00
Note: Family tickets are also available
Programme Price: £3.00

DISABLED INFORMATION

Wheelchairs: 9 spaces in front of Bristow Bench Stand for home supporters plus 9 spaces in the Away end.
Helpers: One helper admitted per wheelchair
Prices: Normal prices for the disabled. Free for helpers
Disabled Toilets: Available in the Ellacombe End and the Away End
Audio facilities are available for the blind from reception
Contact: (01803) 328666 Option 0
(Bookings are necessary for the blind)

Travelling Supporters' Information:
Routes: From the North and East: Take the M5 to the A38 then A380 to Torquay. On entering Torquay, turn left at the 1st set of traffic lights after Riviera Way Retail Park into Hele Road. Following signs for the ground, continue straight on over two mini-roundabouts, go up West Hill Road to the traffic lights, then straight ahead into Warbro Road. The ground is situated on the right after 200 yards.

TRANMERE ROVERS FC

Founded: 1884
Former Name: Belmont FC
Nickname: 'Rovers'
Ground: Prenton Park, Prenton Road West, Birkenhead   CH42 9PY
Ground Capacity: 16,151 (All seats)
Record Attendance: 24,424 (5th February 1972)

Pitch Size: 110 × 70 yards
Colours: White shirts and shorts
Telephone Nº: 03330 144452
Ticket Office: 03330 144452
Fax Number: (0151) 609-0606
Web Site: www.tranmererovers.co.uk
E-mail: customerservice@tranmererovers.co.uk

GENERAL INFORMATION

Car Parking: Large car park at the ground (£5.00 per car)
Coach Parking: At the ground (£10.00 charge)
Nearest Railway Stations: Hamilton Square, Rock Ferry and Conway Park (approximately 1½ miles)
Nearest Bus Station: Conway Park (Town Centre)
Club Shop: At the ground
Opening Times: Weekdays 9.30am–5.00pm, Matchdays 10.00am– kick-off, non-Saturday matchdays 10.00am–1.00pm
Telephone Nº: 03330 144452

GROUND INFORMATION

Away Supporters' Entrances & Sections:
Cowshed Stand turnstiles 5-9 – access from Borough Road (Away section capacity: 2,500)

ADMISSION INFO (2015/2016 PRICES)

Adult Seating: £17.00 – £20.00
Under-12s Seating: £2.00 – £5.00
Under-17s Seating: £5.00 – £6.00
Senior Citizen Seating: £10.00 – £13.00
Young Persons Ticket (Ages 17-22): £10.00 – £13.00
Programme Price: £3.00
Note: Young Person tickets must be purchased from the Ticket Office prior to the game and are only sold upon presentation of photographic proof of age.

DISABLED INFORMATION

Wheelchairs: 40 spaces in total for Home and Away fans in the disabled section, Bebington Paddock
Helpers: One helper admitted per disabled person
Prices: £8.00
Disabled Toilets: 2 available in the disabled section
Contact: 03330 144452   (Bookings are necessary)

Travelling Supporters' Information:
Routes: From the North: From Liverpool city centre, travel through the Kingsway (Wallasey) Mersey Tunnel (£1.70 toll for cars) then continue onto the M53, exiting at Junction 3. Take the first exit (signposted Birkenhead), continue past Sainsbury's then turn right at the traffic lights by the Halfway House pub then turn left into Prenton Road West at the next set of lights. The ground is on the right after a short distance. From the South: Exit the M53 at Junction 4 and take the 4th exit at the roundabout onto the B5151 Mount Road (the ground is signposted from here). After 2½ miles, turn right at the traffic lights (by the United Reformed Church) into Prenton Road West for the ground.

WELLING UNITED FC

Founded: 1963
Former Names: None
Nickname: 'The Wings'
Ground: Park View Road Ground, Welling, Kent, DA16 1SY
Record Attendance: 4,020 (1989/90)
Pitch Size: 112 × 72 yards

Colours: Shirts are Red with White facings, Red shorts
Telephone Nº: (0208) 301-1196
Daytime Phone Nº: (0208) 301-1196
Fax Number: (0208) 301-5676
Ground Capacity: 4,000
Seating Capacity: 500
Web site: www.wellingunited.com

GENERAL INFORMATION

Car Parking: Street parking only
Coach Parking: Outside of the ground
Nearest Railway Station: Welling (¾ mile)
Nearest Bus Station: Bexleyheath
Club Shop: At the ground
Opening Times: Matchdays only
Telephone Nº: (0208) 301-1196

GROUND INFORMATION

Away Supporters' Entrances & Sections:
Accommodation in the Danson Park End

ADMISSION INFO (2015/2016 PRICES)

Adult Standing: £15.00
Adult Seating: £16.00
Concessionary Standing: £9.00 – £10.00
Concessionary Seating: £10.00 – £11.00
Under-12s Standing: Free with a paying adult
Under-12s Seating: £1.00 with a paying adult

DISABLED INFORMATION

Wheelchairs: Accommodated at the side of the Main Stand
Helpers: Admitted
Prices: £7.50 for the disabled. Helpers pay normal prices
Disabled Toilets: Yes
Contact: (0208) 301-1196 (Bookings are not necessary)

Travelling Supporters' Information:
Routes: Take the A2 (Rochester Way) from London, then the A221 Northwards (Danson Road) to Bexleyheath. At the end turn left towards Welling along Park View Road and the ground is on the left.

WOKING FC

Founded: 1889
Former Names: None
Nickname: 'Cardinals'
Ground: Kingfield Stadium, Kingfield, Woking, Surrey GU22 9AA
Record Attendance: 6,000 (1997)
Pitch Size: 109 × 76 yards

Colours: Shirts are Red & White halves, Black shorts
Telephone Nº: (01483) 772470
Daytime Phone Nº: (01483) 772470
Fax Number: (01483) 888423
Ground Capacity: 6,161
Seating Capacity: 2,511
Web site: www.wokingfc.co.uk
E-mail: admin@wokingfc.co.uk

GENERAL INFORMATION

Car Parking: Limited parking at the ground
Coach Parking: Please contact the club for details
Nearest Railway Station: Woking (1 mile)
Nearest Bus Station: Woking
Club Shop: At the ground
Opening Times: Weekdays and Matchdays
Telephone Nº: (01483) 772470

GROUND INFORMATION

Away Supporters' Entrances & Sections:
Kingfield Road entrance for the Tennis Club terrace

ADMISSION INFO (2015/2016 PRICES)

Adult Standing: £18.00
Adult Seating: £18.00
Under-16s/Student Standing: £5.00
Under-16s/Student Seating: £5.00
Senior Citizen Standing: £13.00
Senior Citizen Seating: £13.00

DISABLED INFORMATION

Wheelchairs: 8 spaces in the Leslie Gosden Stand and 8 spaces in front of the Family Stand
Helpers: Admitted
Prices: One wheelchair and helper for £13.00
Disabled Toilets: Yes – in the Leslie Gosden Stand and Family Stand area
Contact: (01483) 772470 (Bookings are necessary)

Travelling Supporters' Information:
Routes: Exit the M25 at Junction 10 and follow the A3 towards Guildford. Leave at the next junction onto the B2215 through Ripley and join the A247 to Woking. Alternatively, exit the M25 at Junction 11 and follow the A320 to Woking Town Centre. The ground is on the outskirts of Woking – follow signs on the A320 and A247.

WREXHAM FC

Founded: 1864
Nickname: 'Red Dragons'
Ground: Racecourse Ground, Mold Road, Wrexham, North Wales LL11 2AH
Ground Capacity: 10,500 (all seats)
Record Attendance: 34,445 (26th January 1957)
Pitch Size: 111 × 71 yards

Colours: Red shirts with White shorts
Telephone Nº: (01978) 891864
Web Site: www.wrexhamafc.co.uk
E-mail: info@wrexhamfc.tv

GENERAL INFORMATION
Car Parking: Town car parks are nearby and also Glyndwr University (Mold End)
Coach Parking: By Police direction
Nearest Railway Station: Wrexham General (adjacent)
Nearest Bus Station: Wrexham (King Street)
Club Shop: At the ground in the Yale Stand
Opening Times: Monday to Saturday 9.00am to 5.00pm
Telephone Nº: (01978) 262129

GROUND INFORMATION
Away Supporters' Entrances & Sections:
Turnstiles 1-4 for the Yale Stand

ADMISSION INFO (2015/2016 PRICES)
Adult Seating: £15.00 – £19.00
Under-16s Seating: £6.00 – £7.00
Under-11s Seating: £1.00 (with a paying adult)
Concessionary Seating: £12.00 – £14.00
Over-80s Seating: £6.00 – £7.00
Note: Family tickets are also available

DISABLED INFORMATION
Wheelchairs: 35 spaces in the Mold Road Stand
Helpers: One helper admitted per wheelchair
Prices: Normal prices for the disabled. Free for helpers
Disabled Toilets: Available in the disabled section
Contact: (01978) 262129 (Bookings are preferred)

Travelling Supporters' Information:
Routes: From the North and West: Take the A483 and the Wrexham bypass to the junction with the A541. Branch left at the roundabout and follow Wrexham signs into Mold Road; From the East: Take the A525 or A534 into Wrexham then follow the A541 signs into Mold Road; From the South: Take the the M6, then the M54 and follow the A5 and A483 to the Wrexham bypass and the junction with the A541. Branch right at the roundabout and follow signs for the Town Centre.

THE VANARAMA NATIONAL LEAGUE NORTH

Address

4th Floor, 20 Waterloo Street, Birmingham B2 5TB

Phone (0121) 643-3143

Web site www.footballconference.co.uk

Clubs for the 2015/2016 Season

AFC Fylde	Page 31
AFC Telford United	Page 32
Alfreton Town FC	Page 33
Boston United FC	Page 34
Brackley Town FC	Page 35
Bradford Park Avenue FC	Page 36
Chorley FC	Page 37
Corby Town FC	Page 38
Curzon Ashton FC	Page 39
FC United of Manchester	Page 40
Gainsborough Trinity FC	Page 41
Gloucester City FC	Page 42
Harrogate Town FC	Page 43
Hednesford Town FC	Page 44
Lowestoft Town FC	Page 45
North Ferriby United FC	Page 46
Nuneaton Town FC	Page 47
Solihull Moors FC	Page 48
Stalybridge Celtic FC	Page 49
Stockport County FC	Page 50
Tamworth FC	Page 51
Worcester City FC	Page 52

AFC FYLDE

Founded: 1988
Former Names: Formed by the amalgamation of Wesham FC and Kirkham Town FC in 1988
Nickname: 'The Coasters'
Ground: Kellamergh Park, Bryning Lane, Warton, Preston PR4 1TN
Record Attendance: 1,418 (13th October 2013)

Colours: White shirts and shorts
Telephone Nº: (01772) 682593
Fax Number: (01772) 685893
Ground Capacity: 3,000
Seating Capacity: 533
Pitch Size: 110 × 82 yards
Web Site: www.afcfylde.co.uk

GENERAL INFORMATION

Car Parking: At the ground
Coach Parking: At the ground
Nearest Railway Station: Moss Side (2¼ miles)
Club Shop: 6 Station Road, Kirkham PR4 2AS
Opening Times: Matchdays only
Telephone Nº: (01772) 682593 (Phone orders accepted)

GROUND INFORMATION

Away Supporters' Entrances & Sections: No usual segregation

ADMISSION INFO (2015/2016 PRICES)

Adult Standing: £12.00
Adult Seating: £12.00
Concessionary Standing: £9.00
Concessionary Seating: £9.00
Student Standing: £5.00
Student Seating: £5.00
Under-16s Standing: Free of charge
Under-16s Seating: Free of charge
Programme Price: £2.00

DISABLED INFORMATION

Wheelchairs: Accommodated
Helpers: Admitted
Prices: Normal prices apply for the disabled. Helpers pay concessionary prices
Disabled Toilets: None
Contact: (01772) 682593 (Bookings are not necessary)

Travelling Supporters' Information:
Routes: Exit the M55 at Junction 3 and take the A585 (signposted Fleetwood/Kirkham). At the roundabout outside of Kirkham, take the 2nd exit continuing on the A585, go straight on at the next roundabout, then at the roundabout junction with the A583, take the 2nd exit onto the B5259 Ribby Road. Follow this road into Wrea Green, then turn left by the Green itself into Bryning Lane. Continue for about 1 mile and the ground is situated on the left of the road.

AFC TELFORD UNITED

Founded: 2004
Former Names: Formed after Telford United FC went out of business. TUFC were previously known as Wellington Town FC
Nickname: 'The Bucks'
Ground: The New Bucks Head Stadium, Watling Street, Wellington, Telford TF1 2TU
Record Attendance: 13,000 (1935)

Pitch Size: 110 × 74 yards
Colours: White shirts and shorts
Telehone N°: (01952) 640064
Fax Number: (01952) 640021
Ground Capacity: 5,780
Seating Capacity: 2,280
Web site: www.telfordunited.com
E-mail: office@telfordutd.co.uk

GENERAL INFORMATION
Car Parking: At the ground (£3.00 charge for cars)
Coach Parking: At the ground
Nearest Railway Station: Wellington
Nearest Bus Station: Wellington
Club Shop: At the ground
Opening Times: Saturday matchdays only from 1.30pm.
Telephone N°: None

GROUND INFORMATION
Away Supporters' Entrances & Sections:
Frank Nagington Stand on the rare occasions when segregation is used

ADMISSION INFO (2015/2016 PRICES)
Adult Standing: £15.00
Adult Seating: £15.00
Under-16s Standing: £2.00
Under-16s Seating: £2.00
Under-20s Standing: £5.00
Under-20s Seating: £5.00
Concessionary Standing: £12.00
Concessionary Seating: £12.00

DISABLED INFORMATION
Wheelchairs: Accommodated at both ends of the ground
Helpers: Admitted
Prices: Normal prices apply
Disabled Toilets: Available by the Sir Stephen Roberts Stand
Contact: (01952) 640064 (Bookings are not necessary)

Travelling Supporters' Information:
Routes: Exit the M54 at Junction 6 and take the A518. Go straight on at the first roundabout, take the second exit at the next roundabout then turn left at the following roundabout. Follow the road round to the right then turn left into the car park.

ALFRETON TOWN FC

Founded: 1959
Former Names: None
Nickname: 'Reds'
Ground: The Impact Arena, North Street, Alfreton, Derbyshire DE55 7FZ
Record Attendance: 5,023 vs Matlock Town (1960)
Pitch Size: 110 × 75 yards

Colours: Red shirts and shorts
Telephone Nº: (0115) 939-2090
Fax Number: (0115) 949-1846
Ground Capacity: 5,100
Seating Capacity: 1,600
Web site: www.alfretontownfc.com

GENERAL INFORMATION
Car Parking: At the ground
Coach Parking: Available close to the ground
Nearest Railway Station: Alfreton (½ mile)
Nearest Bus Station: Alfreton (5 minutes walk)
Club Shop: At the ground
Opening Times: Matchdays only
Telephone Nº: (01773) 830277

GROUND INFORMATION
Away Supporters' Entrances & Sections:
Segregation is usual so please check prior to the game

ADMISSION INFO (2015/2016 PRICES)
Adult Standing: £14.00
Adult Seating: £14.00
Senior Citizen Standing/Seating: £10.00
Ages 16 to 21 Standing/Seating: £10.00
Under-16s Standing: £2.00 (with a paying adult)
Under-16s Seating: £2.00 (with a paying adult)

DISABLED INFORMATION
Wheelchairs: Accommodated in dedicated areas of the ground
Helpers: Admitted
Prices: Please phone the club for information
Disabled Toilets: Available
Contact: (01773) 830277   (Bookings are not necessary)

Travelling Supporters' Information:
Routes: Exit the M1 at Junction 28 and take the A38 signposted for Derby. After 2 miles take the sliproad onto the B600 then go right at the main road towards the town centre. After ½ mile turn left down North Street and the ground is on the right after 200 yards.

BOSTON UNITED FC

Founded: 1933
Former Names: Boston Town FC & Boston Swifts FC
Nickname: 'The Pilgrims'
Ground: Jakeman's Stadium, York Street, Boston, PE21 6JN
Ground Capacity: 6,613 **Seating Capacity**: 2,000
Pitch Size: 112 × 72 yards

Record Attendance: 10,086 (1955)
Colours: Amber and Black shirts, Black shorts
Telephone Nº: (01205) 364406 (Office)
Matchday Info: (01205) 364406 or 07860 663299
Fax Number: (01205) 354063
Web Site: www.bufc.co.uk
E-mail: admin@bufc.co.uk

GENERAL INFORMATION
Car Parking: Permit holders only
Coach Parking: Available near to the ground
Nearest Railway Station: Boston (1 mile)
Nearest Bus Station: Boston Coach Station (¼ mile)
Club Shop: In the car park at the ground
Opening Times: Weekdays from 9.00am to 5.00pm and Saturday Matchdays from 11.00am to 5.00pm
Telephone Nº: (01205) 364406

GROUND INFORMATION
Away Supporters' Entrances & Sections:
York Street Entrances 3 & 4 (subject to a move to the Jakemans Stand if so advised by the police)

ADMISSION INFO (2015/2016 PRICES)
Adult Standing: £12.00
Adult Seating: £14.00
Child Standing: £4.00
Child Seating: £5.00
Senior Citizen Standing: £9.00
Senior Citizen Seating: £10.00

DISABLED INFORMATION
Wheelchairs: 7 spaces available for home fans, 4 spaces for away fans below the Main Stand at the Town End
Helpers: One helper admitted per disabled fan
Prices: £12.00 for the disabled. Free of charge for helpers
Disabled Toilets: Available in the Town End Terrace
Contact: (01205) 364406 (Bookings are necessary)

Travelling Supporters' Information:
From the North: Take the A17 from Sleaford, bear right after the railway crossing to the traffic lights over the bridge. Go forward through the traffic lights into York Street for the ground; From the South: Take the A16 from Spalding and turn right at the traffic lights over the bridge. Go forward through the next traffic lights into York Street for the ground.

BRACKLEY TOWN FC

Founded: 1890
Former Names: None
Nickname: 'Saints'
Ground: St. James Park, Churchill Way, Brackley, NN13 7EJ
Record Attendance: 2,604 (2012/13 season)

Colours: Red and Black striped shirts with Black shorts
Telephone Nº: (01280) 704077
Ground Capacity: 3,500
Seating Capacity: 300
Web Site: www.brackleytownfc.com

GENERAL INFORMATION

Car Parking: At the ground (£2.00 charge per car)
Coach Parking: At the ground
Nearest Railway Station: King's Sutton (6¾ miles)
Club Shop: At the ground
Opening Times: Matchdays and by appointment only
Telephone Nº: (01280) 704077

GROUND INFORMATION

Away Supporters' Entrances & Sections:
No usual segregation

ADMISSION INFO (2015/2016 PRICES)

Adult Standing: £12.00
Adult Seating: £12.00
Senior Citizen/Student Standing: £6.00
Senior Citizen/Student Seating: £6.00
Under-16s Standing: £3.00
Under-16s Seating: £3.00

DISABLED INFORMATION

Wheelchairs: Accommodated
Helpers: Admitted
Prices: Normal prices apply for the disabled and helpers
Disabled Toilets: Available
Contact: (01280) 704077 (Stephen Toghill – bookings are necessary)

Travelling Supporters' Information:
Routes: From the West: Take the A422 to Brackley and take the first exit at the roundabout with the junction of the A43, heading north into Oxford Road.* Go straight on at the next roundabout and continue into Bridge Street before turning right into Churchill Way. The ground is located at the end of the road; From the South: Take the A43 northwards to Brackley. Take the second exit at the roundabout with the junction of the A422 and head into Oxford Road. Then as from * above; From the North-East: Take the A43 to Brackley. Upon reaching Brackley, take the 1st exit at the 1st roundabout, the 2nd exit at the next roundabout then the 3rd exit at the following roundabout into Oxford Road. Then as from * above.

BRADFORD PARK AVENUE FC

Founded: 1907   (Re-formed in 1988)
Former Names: None
Nickname: 'Avenue'
Ground: Horsfall Stadium, Cemetery Road, Bradford, BD6 2NG
Record Attendance: 2,100 (2003)
Pitch Size: 112 × 71 yards

Colours: Green & White striped shirts, White shorts
Telephone N°: 07912 271498 (Ground)
Office Address: Hugh House, Foundry Street, Brighouse   HD6 1LT
Office Number: (01484) 400007
Ground Capacity: 3,000   **Seating Capacity**: 1,247
Web site: www.bpafc.com

GENERAL INFORMATION
Car Parking: Street parking and some spaces at the ground
Coach Parking: At the ground
Nearest Railway Station: Bradford Interchange (3 miles)
Nearest Bus Station: Bradford Interchange (3 miles)
Club Shop: At the ground
Opening Times: Matchdays only
Telephone N°: –

GROUND INFORMATION
Away Supporters' Entrances & Sections: Segregation only used when required

ADMISSION INFO (2015/2016 PRICES)
Adult Standing/Seating: £11.00
Senior Citizen Standing/Seating: £7.00
Student Standing/Seating: £7.00
Under-16s Standing/Seating: £2.00
Armed Forces Standing/Seating: £5.00 (warrant card must be shown)

DISABLED INFORMATION
Wheelchairs: Accommodated in front of the Stand
Helpers: Please phone the club for information
Prices: Please phone the club for information
Disabled Toilets: Available
Contact: –   (Bookings are not necessary)

Travelling Supporters' Information:
Routes: Exit the M62 at Junction 26 and take the M606 to its end. At the roundabout go along the A6036 (signposted Halifax) and pass Odsal Stadium on the left. At the roundabout by Osdal take the 3rd exit (still A6036 Halifax). After just under 1 mile, turn left at the Kinderhaven Nursery into Cemetery Road. The ground is 150 yards on the left.

CHORLEY FC

Founded: 1883
Former Names: None
Nickname: 'Magpies'
Ground: Victory Park Stadium, Duke Street, Chorley, PR7 3DU
Record Attendance: 9,679 (1931/32 season)
Pitch Size: 112 × 72 yards

Colours: Black & White striped shirts with Black shorts
Telephone Nº: (01257) 230007
Fax Number: (01257) 275662
Ground Capacity: 3,550
Seating Capacity: 900
Web site: www.chorleyfc.com
E-mail: info@chorleyfc.com

GENERAL INFORMATION

Car Parking: 80 spaces available at the ground (£3.00)
Coach Parking: At the ground
Nearest Railway Station: Chorley (¼ mile)
Nearest Bus Station: 15 minutes from the ground
Club Shop: At the ground
Opening Times: Matchdays only
Telephone Nº: –

GROUND INFORMATION

Away Supporters' Entrances & Sections:
Pilling Lane Stand entrances and accommodation

ADMISSION INFO (2015/2016 PRICES)

Adult Standing: £10.00
Adult Seating: £10.00
Concessionary Standing/Seating: £7.00
Under-16s Standing/Seating: £5.00
Under-12s Standing/Seating: £2.00
Under-8s Standing/Seating: Free of charge
Programme Price: £2.50

DISABLED INFORMATION

Wheelchairs: Accommodated by prior arrangement
Helpers: Please contact the club for information
Prices: Please contact the club for information
Disabled Toilets: Available in the Social Club
Contact: (01257) 230007 (Bookings are not necessary)

Travelling Supporters' Information:
Routes: Exit the M61 at Junction 6 and follow the A6 to Chorley. Going past the Yarrow Bridge Hotel on Bolton Road, turn left at the 1st set of traffic lights into Pilling Lane. Take the 1st right into Ashby Street and the ground is the 2nd entrance on the left; Alternative Route: Exit the M6 at Junction 27 and follow signs to Chorley. Turn left at the lights and continue down the A49 for 2½ miles before turning right onto B5251. On entering Chorley, turn right into Duke Street 200 yards past The Plough.

CORBY TOWN FC

Photograph courtesy of Chris Rivett, Final Third Sports Media

Founded: 1948
Former Names: None
Nickname: 'The Steelmen'
Ground: Steel Park, Jimmy Kane Way, Rockingham Road, Corby   NN17 2FB
Record Attendance: 2,240 vs Watford (1986/87)
Pitch Size: 111 × 72 yards

Colours: Black and White striped shirts, Black shorts
Telephone Nº: 07932 633343
Ground Capacity: 3,893
Seating Capacity: 577
Web site: www.corbytownfc.co.uk
E-mail: info@corbytownfc.co.uk

GENERAL INFORMATION
Car Parking: Spaces for 190 cars at the ground
Coach Parking: Spaces for 3 coaches at the ground
Nearest Railway Station: Corby (2 miles)
Nearest Bus Station: Corby Town Centre
Club Shop: At the ground
Opening Times: Matchdays only – 1 hour before kick-off
Telephone Nº: 07783 578262

GROUND INFORMATION
Away Supporters' Entrances & Sections:
No usual segregation

ADMISSION INFO (2015/2016 PRICES)
Adult Standing/Seating: £12.00
Senior Citizen Standing/Seating: £8.00
Under-16s Standing/Seating: £2.00

DISABLED INFORMATION
Wheelchairs: Accommodated
Helpers: Admitted
Prices: Normal prices apply for disabled fans. Helpers are admitted free of charge
Disabled Toilets: Available
Contact: (01536) 406640   (Bookings are not necessary)

Travelling Supporters' Information:
Routes: From the North & East: Exit the A1(M) at junction 17 and take the A605 to Oundle then the A427 to Little Weldon. At the roundabout take the A6116 towards Rockingham and the ground is adjacent to Rockingham Castle near the junction with the A6003; From the South: Take the A14 to the junction with the A6116 and continue to the junction with the A6003 at Rockingham Castle; From the West: Take the A14 or A427 to the A6003 then continue north towards Rockingham to the junction with the A6116 where the ground is on the left.

CURZON ASHTON FC

Founded: 1963
Former Names: None
Nickname: 'The Nash'
Ground: Tameside Stadium, Richmond Street, Ashton-under-Lyne OL7 9HG
Record Attendance: 1,826
Pitch Size: 114 × 72 yards

Colours: Royal Blue shirts and shorts
Telephone Nº: (0161) 330-6033
Fax Number: (0161) 339-8802
Ground Capacity: 4,000
Seating Capacity: 527
Web Site: www.curzon-ashton.co.uk

GENERAL INFORMATION
Car Parking: At the ground
Coach Parking: At the ground
Nearest Railway Station: Ashton-under-Lyne (1 mile)
Club Shop: At the ground
Opening Times: Matchdays only
Telephone Nº: (0161) 330-6033

GROUND INFORMATION
Away Supporters' Entrances & Sections:
No usual segregation

ADMISSION INFO (2015/2016 PRICES)
Adult Standing: £10.00
Adult Seating: £10.00
Concessionary Standing: £5.00
Concessionary Seating: £5.00
Under-16s Standing: £3.00
Under-16s Seating: £3.00
Programme Price: £2.00

DISABLED INFORMATION
Wheelchairs: Accommodated
Helpers: Admitted
Prices: Normal prices apply for the disabled and helpers
Disabled Toilets: Available
Contact: (0161) 330-6033   (Bookings are not necessary)

Travelling Supporters' Information:
Routes: Exit the M60 at Junction 23 and take the A6140 signposted for Ashton. Continue along the A6140 to the set of traffic lights with a Cinema on the right then turn left. Cross over a bridge and go straight across the mini-roundabout before turning left into the ground. NOTE: Diversions may be in force during the 2010/2011 season due to bridge replacement work.

FC UNITED OF MANCHESTER

Founded: 2005
Nickname: 'F.C.'
Ground: Broadhurst Park, 310 Lightbowne Road, Moston, Manchester M40 0FJ
Ground Capacity: 4,400
Seating Capacity: 750
Pitch Size: 110 × 71 yards

Record Attendance: 4,232 (29th May 2015)
Colours: Red shirts with White shorts
Telephone Nº: (0161) 769-2005
Fax Number: (0161) 769-2014
E-mail: office@fc-utd.co.uk
Web Site: www.fc-utd.co.uk

GENERAL INFORMATION

Car Parking: None available at the ground. A number of car parks are located within ½ mile of Broadhurst Park. Please check the club's web site for further information.
Coach Parking: Phone the club on (0161) 769-2005
Nearest Railway Station: Moston (¾ mile)
Nearest Bus Station: A number of services travel to the ground. Please check the club's web site for further details.
Club Shop: At the ground
Opening Times: Matchdays only
Telephone Nº: (0161) 769-2005

GROUND INFORMATION

Away Supporters' Entrances & Sections:
No usual segregation but away fans will be accommodated in the Lightbowne Road End if necessary.

ADMISSION INFO (2015/2016 PRICES)

Adult Seating: £9.00
Senior Citizen (Over-60s)/Student Seating: £5.00
Under-18s Seating: £2.00
Programme Price: £2.00

DISABLED INFORMATION

Wheelchairs: Spaces for wheelchairs are available in all areas of the ground
Helpers: One helper admitted per wheelchair
Prices: Normal prices for wheelchair users. Helpers are admitted free of charge.
Disabled Toilets: Available behind the Main Stand
Contact: (0161) 769-2005 (Bookings are not necessary)

Travelling Supporters' Information: From the M60 travelling clockwise: Exit the M60 at junction 20 and turn onto the A664. At the traffic signals turn left onto the A6104. Travel straight on and then at the Greengate roundabout take the 4th exit onto Lightbowne Road, the B6393. Carry straight on for around a half a mile and Broadhurst Park is on your left; From the M60 travelling anti-clockwise: Exit the M60 at junction 22, then straight on to Hollingwood Avenue, the A6104. Travel straight on and then at the Greengate roundabout take the 1st exit onto Lightbowne Road, the B6393. Carry straight on for around a half a mile and Broadhurst Park is on your left.

GAINSBOROUGH TRINITY FC

Founded: 1873
Former Names: None
Nickname: 'The Blues'
Ground: Northolme, Gainsborough, Lincolnshire, DN21 2QW
Record Attendance: 9,760 (1948)
Pitch Size: 111 × 71 yards

Colours: Blue shirts and shorts
Telephone N°: (01427) 611612
Clubhouse Phone N°: (01427) 613688
Fax Number: (01427) 613295
Ground Capacity: 4,340
Seating Capacity: 504
Web site: www.gainsboroughtrinity.com

GENERAL INFORMATION
Car Parking: Opposite the ground (£2.00 charge).
Coach Parking: Available by prior arrangement
Nearest Railway Station: Lea Road (2 miles) and also Gainsborough Central on Saturdays only (½ mile)
Nearest Bus Station: Heaton Street (1 mile)
Club Shop: At the ground
Opening Times: Matchdays only
Telephone N°: (01427) 611612

GROUND INFORMATION
Away Supporters' Entrances & Sections:
No usual segregation

ADMISSION INFO (2015/2016 PRICES)
Adult Standing: £12.00
Adult Seating: £12.00
Concessionary Standing: £8.00
Concessionary Seating: £8.00
Under-16s Standing/Seating: £4.00
Under-5s Standing/Seating: Free of charge

DISABLED INFORMATION
Wheelchairs: Accommodated
Helpers: Please phone the club for information
Prices: Normal prices for the disabled. Free for helpers
Disabled Toilets: Available adjacent to the Main Stand
Contact: (01427) 613295 (Bookings are not necessary)

Travelling Supporters' Information:
Routes: From the North, South and West: Exit the A1 at Blyth services taking the 1st left through to Bawtry. In Bawtry, turn right at the traffic lights onto the A631 straight through to Gainsborough (approx. 11 miles). Go over the bridge to the second set of traffic lights and turn left onto the A159 (Scunthorpe Road). Follow the main road past Tesco on the right through the traffic lights. The ground is situated on right approximately a third of a mile north of the Town Centre; From the East: Take the A631 into Gainsborough and turn right onto the A159. Then as above.

GLOUCESTER CITY FC

Gloucester City are groundsharing with Cheltenham Town FC for the 2015/2016 season.

Founded: 1889 (**Re-formed**: 1980)
Former Names: Gloucester YMCA
Nickname: 'The Tigers'
Ground: Abbey Business Stadium, Whaddon Road, Cheltenham, Gloucestershire GL52 5NA
Ground Capacity: 7,136
Seating Capacity: 4,054

Record Attendance: 8,326 (1956)
Pitch Size: 110 × 72 yards
Colours: Yellow and Black Striped shirts, Black shorts
Telephone Nº: 07813 931781
Web Site: www.gloucestercityafc.com
E-mail: contact@gloucestercityafc.com

GENERAL INFORMATION
Car Parking: Available at the ground.
Coach Parking: At the ground
Nearest Railway Station: Cheltenham Spa (2½ miles)
Nearest Bus Station: Cheltenham Royal Well
Club Shop: At the ground
Opening Times: Matchdays only

GROUND INFORMATION
Away Supporters' Entrances & Sections:
No usual segregation

ADMISSION INFO (2015/2016 PRICES)
Adult Standing: £12.00
Adult Seating: £12.00
Under-18s Standing: Free of charge
Under-18s Seating: Free of charge
Concessionary Standing: £6.00
Concessionary Seating: £6.00

DISABLED INFORMATION
Wheelchairs: Accommodated in front of the Stagecoach West Stand (use main entrance) and in the In 2 Print Stand
Helpers: Admitted free of charge
Prices: Normal prices apply for disabled fans
Disabled Toilets: Available in the In 2 Print Stand, adjacent to the Stagecoach West Stand and in the Social Club
Contact: 07813 931781

Travelling Supporters' Information:
Routes: The ground is situated to the North-East of Cheltenham, 1 mile from the Town Centre off the B4632 (Prestbury Road) – Whaddon Road is to the East of the B4632 just North of Pittville Circus. Road signs in the vicinity indicate 'Whaddon Road/ Cheltenham Town FC'.

HARROGATE TOWN FC

Founded: 1919
Former Names: Harrogate FC and Harrogate Hotspurs FC
Nickname: 'Town'
Ground: CNG Stadium, Wetherby Road, Harrogate, HG2 7SA
Record Attendance: 4,280 (1950)
Pitch Size: 107 × 72 yards

Colours: Yellow and Black striped shirts, Black shorts
Telephone Nº: (01423) 880675
Club Fax Number: (01423) 883671
Ground Capacity: 3,290
Seating Capacity: 502
Web site: www.harrogatetown.com
E-mail: enquiries@harrogatetown.com

GENERAL INFORMATION
Car Parking: Hospital Car Park adjacent
Coach Parking: At the ground
Nearest Railway Station: Harrogate (¾ mile)
Nearest Bus Station: Harrogate
Club Shop: At the ground
Opening Times: Monday to Friday 9.00am to 3.00pm and also on Matchdays
Telephone Nº: (01423) 885525

GROUND INFORMATION
Away Supporters' Entrances & Sections:
No usual segregation

ADMISSION INFO (2015/2016 PRICES)
Adult Standing: £13.00   **Adult Seating**: £14.00
Concessionary Standing: £8.00
Concessionary Seating: £9.00
Student Standing/Seating: £3.00
Under-18s Standing: £3.00
Under-18s Seating: £4.00

DISABLED INFORMATION
Wheelchairs: Accommodated at the front of the Main Stand
Helpers: One helper admitted for each disabled fan
Prices: Free of charge for each disabled fan and helper
Disabled Toilets: Available
Contact: (01423) 880675   (Bookings are necessary)

Travelling Supporters' Information:
Routes: From the South: Take the A61 from Leeds and turn right at the roundabout onto the ring road (signposted York). After about 1¼ miles turn left at the next roundabout onto A661 Wetherby Road. The ground is situated ¾ mile on the right; From the West: Take the A59 straight into Wetherby Road from Empress Roundabout and the ground is on the left; From the East & North: Exit the A1(M) at Junction 47, take the A59 to Harrogate then follow the Southern bypass to Wetherby Road for the A661 Roundabout. Turn right towards Harrogate Town Centre and the ground is on the right after ¾ mile.

HEDNESFORD TOWN FC

Founded: 1880
Former Names: Formed by the amalgamation of West Hill FC and Hill Top FC
Nickname: 'The Pitmen'
Ground: Keys Park, Keys Park Road, Hednesford, Cannock WS12 2DZ
Record Attendance: 4,412 (11th May 2013)

Colours: Black and White shirts with White shorts
Telephone Nº: (01543) 422870
Fax Number: (01543) 428180
Ground Capacity: 6,039
Seating Capacity: 1,011
Pitch Size: 110 × 70 yards
Web site: www.hednesfordtownfc.com

GENERAL INFORMATION
Car Parking: 500 spaces available at the ground – £1.00 fee
Coach Parking: At the ground
Nearest Railway Station: Hednesford (1 mile)
Nearest Bus Station: Hednesford
Club Shop: At the ground
Opening Times: Matchdays and Weekdays from 10.00am to 4.00pm
Telephone Nº: (01543) 422870

GROUND INFORMATION
Away Supporters' Entrances & Sections:
No usual segregation

ADMISSION INFO (2015/2016 PRICES)
Adult Standing: £12.00
Adult Seating: £13.00
Concessionary Standing: £7.00
Concessionary Seating: £8.00
Note: A selection of family tickets are also available
Programme Price: £2.50

DISABLED INFORMATION
Wheelchairs: 8 spaces available in front of the Main Stand
Helpers: Please contact the club for details
Prices: Please contact the club for details
Disabled Toilets: 2 are available – one in the Main Building, one in the Hednesford End of the stand
Contact: (01543) 422870   (Bookings are necessary)

Travelling Supporters' Information:
Routes: Exit the M6 at Junction 11 or the M6 Toll T7 and follow signs for A460 (Rugeley). After crossing the A5 at Churchbridge Island, continue on the A460. After five traffic islands pick up signs for Hednesford Town FC/Keys Park and follow to the ground.

LOWESTOFT TOWN FC

Founded: 1880
Former Names: East Suffolk FC
Nickname: 'The Trawler Boys'
Ground: Crown Meadow, Love Road, Lowestoft, NR32 2PA
Record Attendance: 5,000 (1967)

Colours: Blue shirts and shorts
Telephone Nº: (01502) 573818
Ground Capacity: 3,000
Seating Capacity: 466
Web Site: www.lowestofttownfc.co.uk

GENERAL INFORMATION
Car Parking: Street parking only
Coach Parking: At Lowestoft College
Nearest Railway Station: Lowestoft (½ mile)
Club Shop: At the ground
Opening Times: Matchdays only 11.00am to 5.00pm
Telephone Nº: (01502) 567280

GROUND INFORMATION
Away Supporters' Entrances & Sections: No usual segregation

ADMISSION INFO (2015/2016 PRICES)
Adult Standing: £12.00
Adult Seating: £12.00
Senior Citizen Standing: £9.00
Senior Citizen Seating: £9.00
Under-16s Standing: £3.00
Under-16s Seating: £3.00
Programme Price: £2.00

DISABLED INFORMATION
Wheelchairs: Accommodated
Helpers: Admitted
Prices: Concessionary prices apply for both the disabled and helpers
Disabled Toilets: Available
Contact: 07930 872947 (Bookings are necessary)

Travelling Supporters' Information:
Routes: Take the A146 or the A12 to Lowestoft Town Centre then head north on the A12 Katwijk Way Road. Turn left into Love Road for the ground.

NORTH FERRIBY UNITED FC

Founded: 1934
Former Names: None
Nickname: 'Villagers' or 'Green & Whites'
Ground: Eon Visual Media Stadium, Church Road, North Ferriby, East Yorkshire HU14 3AB
Record Attendance: 2,232 (vs Hull City in 2013)
Pitch Size: 109 × 76 yards

Colours: White shirts with Green trim, Green shorts
Telephone Nº: (01482) 634601
Fax Number: (01482) 634601
Ground Capacity: 3,000
Seating Capacity: 500
Web site: www.northferriby united.com
E-mail: info@northferribyunitedfc.co.uk

GENERAL INFORMATION
Car Parking: Limited spaces at the ground
Coach Parking: At the ground
Nearest Railway Station: Ferriby (5 minutes walk)
Nearest Bus Station: Hull
Club Shop: At the ground
Opening Times: Matchdays only
Telephone Nº: (01482) 634601

GROUND INFORMATION
Away Supporters' Entrances & Sections:
No usual segregation

ADMISSION INFO (2015/2016 PRICES)
Adult Standing: £12.00
Adult Seating: £12.00
Senior Citizen/Under-16s Standing: £6.00
Senior Citizen/Under-16s Seating: £6.00
Programme Price: £2.00

DISABLED INFORMATION
Wheelchairs: Accommodated
Helpers: Admitted
Prices: Standard prices apply
Disabled Toilets: Available
Contact: (01482) 634601 (Bookings are not necessary)

Travelling Supporters' Information:
Routes: North Ferriby is approximately 8 miles to the west of Hull on the A63. Upon reaching North Ferriby (from the West), proceed through the village past the Duke of Cumberland Hotel and turn right into Church Lane. The ground is situated on the left after half a mile.

NUNEATON TOWN FC

Founded: 1937 (Reformed 2008)
Former Names: Nuneaton Borough FC
Nickname: 'Boro'
Ground: Liberty Way, Attleborough Fields Industrial Estate, Nuneaton CV11 6RR
Record Attendance: 3,111 (2nd May 2009)
Pitch Size: 109 × 74 yards

Colours: Blue shirts and white shorts
Telephone Nº: (024) 7638-5738
Fax Number: (024) 7637-2995
Ground Capacity: 4,500
Seating Capacity: 500
Web site: www.nuneatontownfc.com
E-mail: admin@nuneatontownfc.com

GENERAL INFORMATION

Car Parking: On-site car park plus various other parking spaces available on the nearby Industrial Estate (£2.00 fee)
Coach Parking: At the ground (£10.00 fee)
Nearest Railway Station: Nuneaton (2 miles)
Nearest Bus Station: Nuneaton (2 miles)
Club Shop: Yes – The Boro Shop
Opening Times: By appointment and also on matchdays
Telephone Nº: (024) 7638-5738

GROUND INFORMATION

Away Supporters' Entrances & Sections:
No usual segregation

ADMISSION INFO (2015/2016 PRICES)

Adult Standing: £13.00
Adult Seating: £13.00
Concessionary Standing: £13.00
Concessionary Seating: £13.00
Ages 11 to 17 Standing/Seating: £3.00
Under-11s Standing Seating: Free with a paying adult

DISABLED INFORMATION

Wheelchairs: Accommodated, but only 5 spaces are available
Helpers: Admitted
Prices: Normal prices apply for the disabled and helpers
Disabled Toilets: Available
Contact: (024) 7638-5738 (Bookings are necessary)

Travelling Supporters' Information:
Routes: From the South, West and North-West: Exit the M6 at Junction 3 and follow the A444 into Nuneaton. At the Coton Arches roundabout turn right into Avenue Road which is the A4254 signposted for Hinckley. Continue along the A4254 following the road into Garrett Street then Eastboro Way then turn left into Townsend Drive. Follow the road round before turning left into Liberty Way for the ground; From the North: Exit the M1 at Junction 21 and follow the M69. Exit the M69 at Junction 1 and take the 4th exit at the roundabout onto the A5 (Tamworth, Nuneaton). At Longshoot Junction, turn left onto the A47, continue to the roundabout and take the 1st exit onto A4254 Eastborough Way. Turn right at the next roundabout into Townsend Drive then immediately right again for Liberty Way.

SOLIHULL MOORS FC

Photo courtesy of Jordan Martin Photography

Founded: 2007
Former Names: Formed by the merger of Solihull Borough FC and Moor Green FC in 2007
Nickname: 'The Moors'
Ground: The Autotech Stadium, Damson Park, Damson Parkway, Solihull   B91 2PP
Record Attendance: 2,000 (vs Birmingham City)
Pitch Size: 114 × 76 yards

Colours: Yellow and Blue hooped shirts, Blue shorts
Telephone Nº: (0121) 705-6770
Fax Number: (0121) 711-4045
Ground Capacity: 3,300
Seating Capacity: 500
Web site: www.solihullmoorsfc.co.uk
E-mail: solihullfootball@btconnect.com

GENERAL INFORMATION
Car Parking: At the ground
Coach Parking: At the ground
Nearest Railway Station: Birmingham International (2 miles)
Nearest Bus Station: Birmingham (5 miles)
Club Shop: At the ground
Opening Times: Matchdays only
Telephone Nº: (0121) 705-6770

GROUND INFORMATION
Away Supporters' Entrances & Sections:
No usual segregation

ADMISSION INFO (2015/2016 PRICES)
Adult Standing: £10.00
Adult Seating: £10.00
Senior Citizen/Junior Standing: £5.00
Senior Citizen/Junior Seating: £5.00
Note: Under-12s are admitted free of charge when accompanied by a paying adult

DISABLED INFORMATION
Wheelchairs: Spaces for 3 wheelchairs are available
Helpers: Admitted
Prices: Normal prices apply
Disabled Toilets: Available
Contact: (0121) 705-6770

Travelling Supporters' Information:
Routes: Exit the M42 at Junction 6 and take the A45 for 2 miles towards Birmingham. Turn left at the traffic lights near the Posthouse Hotel into Damson Parkway (signposted for Landrover/Damsonwood). Continue to the roundabout and come back along the other carriageway to the ground which is situated on the left after about 150 yards.

STALYBRIDGE CELTIC FC

Founded: 1909
Former Names: None
Nickname: 'Celtic'
Ground: Bower Fold, Mottram Road, Stalybridge, Cheshire SK15 2RT
Record Attendance: 9,753 (1922/23)
Pitch Size: 109 × 70 yards

Colours: Blue shirts, White shorts and Blue socks
Telephone Nº: (0161) 338-2828
Fax Number: (0161) 338-8256
Ground Capacity: 6,108
Seating Capacity: 1,155
Web site: www.stalybridgeceltic.co.uk
E-mail: office@stalybridgeceltic.co.uk

GENERAL INFORMATION

Car Parking: At the ground (£1.00 charge)
Coach Parking: At the ground
Nearest Railway Station: Stalybridge (1 mile)
Nearest Bus Station: Stalybridge town centre
Club Shop: At the ground and also at "Stitch in Time", Market Street, Stalybridge
Opening Times: Matchdays only at the ground Monday to Friday 9.00am to 5.00pm at Market Street
Telephone Nº: (0161) 338-2828

GROUND INFORMATION

Away Supporters' Entrances & Sections:
Lockwood & Greenwood Stand on the few occasions when segregation is required. No usual segregation

ADMISSION INFO (2015/2016 PRICES)

Adult Standing: £12.00
Adult Seating: £12.00
Concessionary Standing: £7.00
Concessionary Seating: £7.00
Note: Under-14s are admitted for £1.00 when accompanied by a paying adult

DISABLED INFORMATION

Wheelchairs: 20 spaces available each for home and away fans at the side of the Stepan Stand. A further 9 spaces available in the new Lord Tom Pendry Stand
Helpers: Please phone the club for information
Prices: Please phone the club for information
Disabled Toilets: Available at the rear of the Stepan Stand and at the side of the Lord Tom Pendry Stand
Contact: (0161) 338-2828 (Bookings are necessary)

Travelling Supporters' Information:
Routes: From the Midlands and South: Take the M6, M56, M60 and M67, leaving at the end of the motorway. Go across the roundabout to the traffic lights and turn left. The ground is approximately 2 miles on the left before the Hare & Hounds pub; From the North: Exit the M62 at Junction 18 onto the M60 singposted for Ashton-under-Lyne. Follow the M60 to Junction 24 and join the M67, then as from the Midlands and South.

STOCKPORT COUNTY FC

Founded: 1883
Former Names: Heaton Norris Rovers FC
Nickname: 'Hatters' 'County'
Ground: Edgeley Park, Hardcastle Road, Edgeley, Stockport   SK3 9DD
Ground Capacity: 10,641 (All seats)
Record Attendance: 27,833 (11th February 1950)
Pitch Size: 111 × 72 yards

Colours: Blue shirts with White shorts
Telephone Nº: (0161) 286-8888
Ticket Office: (0161) 286-8888 Extension 251
Web Site: www.stockportcounty.com
E-mail: info@stockportcounty.com

GENERAL INFORMATION
Car Parking: Booth Street (nearby) £4.00
Coach Parking: Booth Street (£20.00)
Nearest Railway Station: Stockport (5 minutes walk)
Nearest Bus Station: Mersey Square (10 minutes walk)
Club Shop: At the ground
Opening Times: Monday to Friday from 12.00pm–4.00pm. Open until 7.30pm on matchdays during the week and also on Saturday matchdays 10.00am – 3.00pm then for 30 minutes after the game.
Telephone Nº: (0161) 286-8888 Extension 251

GROUND INFORMATION
Away Supporters' Entrances & Sections:
Railway End turnstiles for Railway End or turnstiles for Popular Side depending on the opponents

ADMISSION INFO (2015/2016 PRICES)
Adult Seating: £15.00
Under-22s Seating: £10.00
Under-18s Seating: £5.00
Senior Citizen Seating: £10.00
Note: Children under the age of 6 are admitted free.

DISABLED INFORMATION
Wheelchairs: 16 spaces in total. 10 in the Hardcastle Road Stand, 6 in the Cheadle Stand
Helpers: One helper admitted per disabled fan
Prices: £10.00 for the disabled. Helpers free of charge
Disabled Toilets: Yes
Contact: (0161) 286-8888 Ext. 251 (Bookings are necessary)

Travelling Supporters' Information:
Routes: From the North, South and West: Exit the M60 at Junction 1 and join the A560, following signs for Cheadle. After ¼ mile turn right into Edgeley Road and after 1 mile turn right into Caroline Street for the ground; From the East: Take the A6 or A560 into Stockport Town Centre and turn left into Greek Street. Take the 2nd exit into Mercian Way (from the roundabout) then turn left into Caroline Street – the ground is straight ahead.

TAMWORTH FC

Founded: 1933
Former Names: None
Nickname: 'The Lambs'
Ground: The Lamb Ground, Kettlebrook, Tamworth, B77 1AA
Record Attendance: 4,920 (3rd April 1948)
Pitch Size: 110 × 73 yards

Colours: Red shirts with Black shorts
Telephone N°: (01827) 65798
Fax Number: (01827) 62236
Ground Capacity: 4,118
Seating Capacity: 520
Web site: www.thelambs.co.uk

GENERAL INFORMATION

Car Parking: 200 spaces available at the ground – £2.00 per car, £5.00 for per minibus or £10.00 per coach
Coach Parking: At the ground
Nearest Railway Station: Tamworth (½ mile)
Nearest Bus Station: Tamworth (½ mile)
Club Shop: At the ground
Opening Times: Weekdays from 10.00am to 4.00pm and also on Matchdays
Telephone N°: (01827) 65798 Option 3

GROUND INFORMATION

Away Supporters' Entrances & Sections:
Gates 1 and 2 for Terracing, Gate 2A for seating

ADMISSION INFO (2015/2016 PRICES)

Adult Standing: £12.00
Adult Seating: £14.00
Under-18s Standing: £4.00
Under-18s Seating: £6.00
Under-16s Standing: £2.00 (Under-5s free)
Under-16s Seating: £4.00
Under-5s Seating: £2.00
Senior Citizen Standing: £7.00
Senior Citizen Seating: £9.00

DISABLED INFORMATION

Wheelchairs: Accommodated
Helpers: Admitted
Prices: Normal prices apply for Wheelchair disabled. Helpers are charged concessionary rates
Disabled Toilets: Yes
Contact: (01827) 65798 (Bookings are advisable)

Travelling Supporters' Information:
Routes: Exit the M42 at Junction 10 and take the A5/A51 to the town centre following signs for Town Centre/Snowdome. The follow signs for Kettlebrook and the ground is in Kettlebrook Road, 50 yards from the traffic island by the Railway Viaduct and the Snowdome. The ground is signposted from all major roads.

WORCESTER CITY FC

Worcester City FC are groundsharing with Kidderminster Harriers FC during the 2015/2016 season.

Founded: 1902
Former Names: Berwick Rangers FC
Nickname: 'The City'
Ground: Aggborough, Hoo Road, Kidderminster, Worcestershire DY10 1NB
Ground Capacity: 6,444
Seating Capacity: 3,143
Record Attendance: 9,155 (1948)

Pitch Size: 110 × 72 yards
Colours: Blue and White striped shirts, Blue shorts
Office Address: Unit 7, Ball Mill Top Business Park, Hallow, Worcester WR2 6LS
Telephone Nº: 0783 708-6205
Fax Number: (01562) 827329 (Kidderminster)
Web site: www.worcestercityfc.com
E-mail: office@worcestercityfc.com

GENERAL INFORMATION
Car Parking: At the ground
Coach Parking: As directed
Nearest Railway Station: Kidderminster
Nearest Bus Station: Kidderminster Town Centre
Club Shop: Online sales only at present
Telephone Nº: (01905) 23003

GROUND INFORMATION
Away Supporters' Entrances & Sections:
John Smiths Stand Entrance D and South Terrace Entrance E

ADMISSION INFO (2015/2016 PRICES)
Adult Standing/Seating: £13.00
Under-16s Standing/Seating: £3.00
Young Adult Standing/Seating: £6.00
Senior Citizen Standing/Seating: £9.00

DISABLED INFORMATION
Wheelchairs: Home fans accommodated at the front of the Main Stand, Away fans in front of the John Smiths Stand
Helpers: Admitted
Prices: Normal prices for the disabled. Free for helpers
Disabled Toilets: Available by the disabled area
Contact: 0783 708-6205 (Bookings are necessary)

Travelling Supporters' Information:
Routes: Exit the M5 at Junction 3 and follow the A456 to Kidderminster. The ground is situated close by the Severn Valley Railway Station so follow the brown Steam Train signs and turn into Hoo Road about 200 yards downhill of the station. Follow the road along for ¼ mile and the ground is on the left.

THE VANARAMA NATIONAL LEAGUE SOUTH

Address

4th Floor, 20 Waterloo Street, Birmingham B2 5TB

Phone (0121) 643-3143

Web site www.footballconference.co.uk

Clubs for the 2015/2016 Season

Basingstoke Town FC	Page 54
Bath City FC	Page 55
Bishop's Stortford FC	Page 56
Chelmsford City FC	Page 57
Concord Rangers FC	Page 58
Dartford FC	Page 59
Eastbourne Borough FC	Page 60
Ebbsfleet United FC	Page 61
Gosport Borough FC	Page 62
Havant & Waterlooville FC	Page 63
Hayes & Yeading United FC	Page 64
Hemel Hempstead Town FC	Page 65
Maidenhead United FC	Page 66
Maidstone United FC	Page 67
Margate FC	Page 68
Oxford City FC	Page 69
St. Albans City FC	Page 70
Sutton United FC	Page 71
Truro City FC	Page 72
Wealdstone FC	Page 73
Weston-super-Mare FC	Page 74
Whitehawk FC	Page 75

BASINGSTOKE TOWN FC

Founded: 1896
Former Names: None
Nickname: 'Dragons'
Ground: The Camrose Ground, Western Way, Basingstoke, Hants. RG22 6EZ
Record Attendance: 5,085 (25th November 1997)
Pitch Size: 110 × 70 yards

Colours: Yellow and Blue shirts with Blue shorts
Telephone Nº: (01256) 327575
Fax Number: (01256) 326346
Social Club Nº: (01256) 464353
Ground Capacity: 6,000
Seating Capacity: 650
Web site: www.basingstoketown.net
E-mail: richard.trodd@ntlworld.com

GENERAL INFORMATION

Car Parking: 600 spaces available at the ground (£1.00)
Coach Parking: Ample room available at ground
Nearest Railway Station: Basingstoke
Nearest Bus Station: Basingstoke Town Centre (2 miles)
Club Shop: The Camrose Shop
Opening Times: Matchdays only
Telephone Nº: (01256) 327575

GROUND INFORMATION

Away Supporters' Entrances & Sections:
No usual segregation

ADMISSION INFO (2015/2016 PRICES)

Adult Standing: £12.00
Adult Seating: £13.00
Concessionary Standing: £8.00
Concessionary Seating: £9.00
Under-16s Standing: £4.00
Under-16s Seating: £5.00
Under-11s Standing: £2.00
Under-11s Seating: £3.00

DISABLED INFORMATION

Wheelchairs: 6 spaces are available under cover
Helpers: Admitted
Prices: Normal prices for the disabled. Free for helpers
Disabled Toilets: Yes
Contact: (01256) 327575 (Bookings are not necessary)

Travelling Supporters' Information:
Routes: Exit the M3 at Junction 6 and take the 1st left at the Black Dam roundabout. At the next roundabout take the 2nd exit, then the 1st exit at the following roundabout and the 5th exit at the next roundabout. This takes you into Western Way and the ground is 50 yards on the right.

BATH CITY FC

Founded: 1889
Former Names: Bath AFC, Bath Railway FC and Bath Amateurs FC
Nickname: 'The Romans'
Ground: Twerton Park, Bath   BA2 1DB
Record Attendance: 18,020 (1960)
Pitch Size: 110 × 76 yards

Colours: Black and White striped shirts, Black shorts
Telephone Nº: (01225) 423087
Ground Capacity: 8,840
Seating Capacity: 1,026
Web site: www.bathcityfc.com
E-mail: info@bathcityfootballclub.co.uk

GENERAL INFORMATION

Car Parking: 150 spaces available at the ground
Coach Parking: Available at the ground
Nearest Railway Station: Oldfield Park (1 mile)
Nearest Bus Station: Dorchester Street, Bath
Club Shop: Yes – contact Andy Weeks, c/o Club
Opening Times: Matchdays and office hours
Telephone Nº: (01225) 313247

GROUND INFORMATION

Away Supporters' Entrances & Sections:
Turnstiles 17-19

ADMISSION INFO (2015/2016 PRICES)

Adult Standing: £12.00
Adult Seating: £13.00
Senior Citizen Standing: £8.00
Senior Citizen Seating: £9.00
Students/Under-18s Standing: £6.00 (**Under-16s** £3.00)
Students/Under-18s Seating: £7.00 (**Under-16s** £4.00)

DISABLED INFORMATION

Wheelchairs: 10 spaces available each for home and away fans in front of the Family Stand
Helpers: Admitted
Prices: Normal prices for the disabled. Free for helpers
Disabled Toilets: Available behind the Family Stand
Contact: (01225) 313247   (Bookings are necessary)

Travelling Supporters' Information:
Route: As a recommendation, avoid exiting the M4 at Junction 18 as the road takes you through Bath City Centre. Instead, exit the M4 at Junction 19 onto the M32. Turn off the M32 at Junction 1 and follow the A4174 Bristol Ring Road south then join the A4 for Bath. On the A4, after passing through Saltford you will reach a roundabout shortly before entering Bath. Take the 2nd exit at this roundabout then follow the road before turning left into Newton Road at the bottom of the steep hill. The ground is then on the right hand side of the road.

BISHOP'S STORTFORD FC

Founded: 1874
Former Names: None
Nickname: 'Blues' 'Bishops'
Ground: Woodside Park, Dunmow Road, Bishop's Stortford CM23 5RG
Record Attendance: 3,555 (2000)
Pitch Size: 110 × 70 yards

Colours: Blue and White shirts with Blue shorts
Telephone Nº: (01279) 306456
Fax Number: (01279) 715621
Ground Capacity: 4,000
Seating Capacity: 225
Web site: www.bsfc.co.uk

GENERAL INFORMATION
Car Parking: 500 spaces available at the ground
Coach Parking: At the ground
Nearest Railway Station: Bishop's Stortford
Nearest Bus Station: Bishop's Stortford
Club Shop: At the ground
Opening Times: Matchdays only 1.30pm to 5.00pm
Telephone Nº: (01279) 306456

GROUND INFORMATION
Away Supporters' Entrances & Sections:
No usual segregation

ADMISSION INFO (2015/2016 PRICES)
Adult Standing/Seating: £12.00
Concessionary Standing/Seating: £7.00
Student Standing/Seating: £6.00
Under-16s Standing/Seating: £5.00
Note: Under-12s are admitted free of charge when accompanied by a paying adult.

DISABLED INFORMATION
Wheelchairs: Accommodated in the disabled section
Helpers: Admitted
Prices: Free of charge for the disabled and helpers
Disabled Toilets: Yes
Contact: (01279) 306456   (Bookings are not necessary)

Travelling Supporters' Information:
Routes: Exit the M11 at junction 8 and take the A1250 towards Bishop Stortford. Turn left at the first roundabout and the ground is first right opposite the Golf Club (the entrance is between Industrial Units).

CHELMSFORD CITY FC

Founded: 1938
Former Names: Chelmsford FC
Nickname: 'City' or 'Clarets'
Ground: Melbourne Stadium, Salerno Way, Chelmsford   CM1 2EH
Record Attendance: 16,807 (at previous ground)
Pitch Size: 109 × 70 yards

Colours: Claret and White shirts and shorts
Telephone Nº: (01245) 290959
Ground Capacity: 3,000
Seating Capacity: 1,400
Web site: www.chelmsfordcityfc.com

GENERAL INFORMATION

Car Parking: Limited space at ground and street parking
Coach Parking: Two spaces available at the ground subject to advance notice
Nearest Railway Station: Chelmsford (2 miles)
Nearest Bus Station: Chelmsford (2 miles)
Club Shop: At the ground
Opening Times: Matchdays only at present
Telephone Nº: (01245) 290959

GROUND INFORMATION

Away Supporters' Entrances & Sections:
No usual segregation

ADMISSION INFO (2015/2016 PRICES)

Adult Standing: £13.00
Adult Seating: £13.00
Under-18s Standing: £5.00
Under-18s Seating: £5.00
Under-12s Standing: Free of charge
Under-12s Seating: Free of charge
Concessionary Standing: £9.00
Concessionary Seating: £9.00

DISABLED INFORMATION

Wheelchairs: Spaces for 11 wheelchairs available
Helpers: Admitted free of charge
Prices: Disabled fans are charged standing admission prices
Disabled Toilets: Available
Contact: (01245) 290959   (Bookings are necessary)

Travelling Supporters' Information:
Route: The ground is situated next to the only set of high rise flats in Chelmsford which can therefore be used as a landmark. From the A12 from London: Exit the A12 at Junction 15 signposted for Chelmsford/Harlow/A414 and head towards Chelmsford along the dual-carriageway. At the third roundabout, immediately after passing the 'Superbowl' on the left, take the first exit into Westway, signposted for the Crematorium and Widford Industrial Estate. Continue along Westway which becomes Waterhouse Lane after the second set of traffic lights. At the next set of lights (at the gyratory system) take the first exit into Rainsford Road, signposted for Sawbridgeworth A1060. Continue along Rainsford Road then turn right into Chignal Road at the second set of traffic lights. Turn right again into Melbourne Avenue and Salerno Way is on the left at the end of the football pitches.

CONCORD RANGERS FC

Founded: 1967
Former Names: None
Nickname: 'The Beachboys'
Ground: Aspect Arena, Thames Road, Canvey Island, SS8 0HH
Record Attendance: 1,800

Colours: Yellow shirts with Yellow shorts
Telephone Nº: (01268) 515750
Ground Capacity: 3,000
Seating Capacity: 340
Web Site: www.concordrangers.co.uk

GENERAL INFORMATION
Car Parking: At the ground
Coach Parking: At the ground
Nearest Railway Station: Benfleet
Club Shop: Available via the club's web site shortly
Opening Times: –
Telephone Nº: –

GROUND INFORMATION
Away Supporters' Entrances & Sections:
No usual segregation

ADMISSION INFO (2015/2016 PRICES)
Adult Standing: £10.00
Adult Seating: £10.00
Senior Citizen Standing: £5.00
Senior Citizen Seating: £5.00
Under-16s Standing/Seating: £3.00
Under-10s Standing/Seating: Free of charge

DISABLED INFORMATION
Wheelchairs: Accommodated
Helpers: Admitted
Prices: Normal prices apply for the disabled and helpers
Disabled Toilets: Available
Contact: (01268) 515750   (Bookings are necessary)

Travelling Supporters' Information:
Routes: Take the A13 to the A130 (Canvey Way) for Canvey Island. At the Benfleet roundabout, take the 3rd exit into Canvey Road and continue along through Charfleets Service Road into Long Road. Take the 5th turn on the right into Thorney Bay Road and Thames Road is the 3rd turn on the right. The ground is on the left-hand side around 300 yards down Thames Road.

DARTFORD FC

Founded: 1888
Former Names: None
Nickname: 'The Darts'
Ground: Princes Park Stadium, Grassbanks, Darenth Road, Dartford   DA1 1RT
Record Attendance: 4,097 (11th November 2006)
Pitch Size: 110 × 71 yards

Colours: White Shirts with Black Shorts
Telephone Nº: (01322) 299990
Fax Number: (01322) 299996
Ground Capacity: 4,118
Seating Capacity: 640
Web Site: www.dartfordfc.co.uk
E-mail: info@dartfordfc.co.uk

GENERAL INFORMATION

Car Parking: At the ground
Coach Parking: At the ground
Nearest Railway Station: Dartford (½ mile)
Nearest Bus Station: Dartford (½ mile) & Bluewater (2 miles)
Club Shop: At the ground
Opening Times: Matchdays only – 1.00pm to 6.00pm (but the stadium itself is open daily).
Telephone Nº: (01322) 299990

ADMISSION INFO (2015/2016 PRICES)

Adult Standing: £14.00
Adult Seating: £14.00
Senior Citizen/Concessionary Standing: £7.00
Senior Citizen/Concessionary Seating: £7.00
Youth (Ages 13 to 17) Standing/Seating: £5.00
Junior (Ages 5 to 12) Standing/Seating: £2.00
Under-5s Standing/Seating: Free of charge

DISABLED INFORMATION

Wheelchairs: Accommodated
Helpers: Admitted
Prices: Concessionary prices for the disabled and helpers
Disabled Toilets: Available
Contact: (01322) 299991   (Bookings are not necessary)

Travelling Supporters' Information:
Routes: From M25 Clockwise: Exit the M25 at Junction 1B. At the roundabout, take the 3rd exit onto Princes Road (A225) then the second exit at the next roundabout.* Continue downhill to the traffic lights (with the ground on the left), turn left into Darenth Road then take the 2nd left for the Car Park; From M25 Anti-clockwise: Exit the M25 at Junction 2 and follow the A225 to the roundabout. Take the first exit at this roundabout then the 2nd exit at the next roundabout. Then as from * above.

EASTBOURNE BOROUGH FC

Founded: 1963
Former Names: Langney Sports FC
Nickname: 'The Sports'
Ground: Langney Sports Club, Priory Lane, Langney, Eastbourne BN23 7QH
Record Attendance: 3,770 (5th November 2005)
Pitch Size: 115 × 72 yards

Colours: Red shirts with Black shorts
Telephone Nº: (01323) 766265
Fax Number: (01323) 741627
Ground Capacity: 4,400
Seating Capacity: 542
Web site: www.ebfc.co.uk

GENERAL INFORMATION

Car Parking: Around 400 spaces available at the ground
Coach Parking: At the ground
Nearest Railway Station: Pevensey & Westham (1½ miles but no public transport to the ground)
Nearest Bus Station: Eastbourne (Service 6A to ground)
Club Shop: At the ground
Opening Times: Matchdays only
Telephone Nº: (01323) 766265

GROUND INFORMATION

Away Supporters' Entrances & Sections:
No usual segregation

ADMISSION INFO (2015/2016 PRICES)

Adult Standing: £12.00
Adult Seating: £12.00
Under-16s Standing: £1.00
Under-16s Seating: £1.00
Senior Citizen Standing: £8.00
Senior Citizen Seating: £8.00

DISABLED INFORMATION

Wheelchairs: 6 spaces available
Helpers: Admitted
Prices: Normal prices apply
Disabled Toilets: Available
Contact: (01323) 766265 (Bookings are necessary)

Travelling Supporters' Information:
Routes: From the North: Exit the A22 onto the Polegate bypass, signposted A27 Eastbourne, Hastings & Bexhill. *Take the 2nd exit at the next roundabout for Stone Cross and Westham (A22) then the first exit at the following roundabout signposted Stone Cross and Westham. Turn right after ½ mile into Friday Street (B2104). At the end of Friday Street, turn left at the double mini-roundabout into Hide Hollow (B2191), passing Eastbourne Crematorium on your right. Turn right at the roundabout into Priory Road, and Priory Lane is about 200 yards down the road on the left; Approaching on the A27 from Brighton: Turn left at the Polegate traffic lights then take 2nd exit at the large roundabout to join the bypass. Then as from *.

EBBSFLEET UNITED FC

Founded: 1946
Former Names: Gravesend & Northfleet United FC, Gravesend United FC and Northfleet United FC
Nickname: 'The Fleet'
Ground: Stonebridge Road, Northfleet, Gravesend, Kent   DA11 9GN
Record Attendance: 12,063 (1963)
Pitch Size: 112 × 72 yards

Colours: Reds shirts with White shorts
Telephone Nº: (01474) 533796
Fax Number: (01474) 324754
Ground Capacity: 5,258
Seating Capacity: 1,220
Web site: www.ebbsfleetunited.co.uk
E-mail: info@eufc.co.uk

GENERAL INFORMATION

Car Parking: Ebbsfleet International Car Park C (when available) and also street parking
Coach Parking: At the ground
Nearest Railway Station: Northfleet (5 minutes walk)
Nearest Bus Station: Bus Stop outside the ground
Club Shop: At the ground
Opening Times: Matchdays only
Telephone Nº: (01474) 533796

GROUND INFORMATION

Away Supporters' Entrances & Sections:
Only some games are segregated – contact club for details

ADMISSION INFO (2015/2016 PRICES)

Adult Standing: £11.00
Adult Seating: £11.00
Concessionary Standing: £9.00
Concessionary Seating: £9.00
Under-16s Standing/Seating: £5.00
Under-12s Standing/Seating: Free of charge when accompanied by a paying adult.

DISABLED INFORMATION

Wheelchairs: 6 spaces are available in the Disabled Area in front of the Main Stand
Helpers: Admitted free of charge
Prices: Please phone the club for information
Disabled Toilets: Available in the Main Stand
Contact: (01474) 533796   (Bookings are necessary)

Travelling Supporters' Information:
Routes: Take the A2 to the Northfleet/Southfleet exit and follow signs for Northfleet (B262). Go straight on at the first roundabout then take the 2nd exit at the 2nd roundabout into Thames Way and follow the football signs for the ground.

GOSPORT BOROUGH FC

Founded: 1944
Former Names: Gosport Borough Athletic FC
Nickname: 'The Boro'
Ground: Privett Park, Privett Road, Gosport, PO12 3SX
Record Attendance: 4,770 (1951)

Colours: Yellow shirts with Navy Blue shorts
Telephone Nº: (023) 9250-1042
Fax Number: (01329) 235961
Ground Capacity: 4,500
Seating Capacity: 450
Web Site: www.gosportboroughfc.co.uk

GENERAL INFORMATION
Car Parking: At the ground
Coach Parking: At the ground
Nearest Railway Station: Fareham (5½ miles)
Club Shop: At the ground
Opening Times: Matchdays only
Telephone Nº: –

GROUND INFORMATION
Away Supporters' Entrances & Sections:
No usual segregation

ADMISSION INFO (2015/2016 PRICES)
Adult Standing: £13.00
Adult Seating: £13.00
Concessionary Standing: £9.00
Concessionary Seating: £9.00
Under-18s Standing/Seating: £5.00
Note: Under-12s are admitted free of charge when accompanied by a paying adult

DISABLED INFORMATION
Wheelchairs: Accommodated
Helpers: Admitted
Prices: Normal prices apply for the disabled and helpers
Disabled Toilets: Available
Contact: (023) 9250-1042 (Bookings are not necessary)

Travelling Supporters' Information:
Routes: Exit the M27 at Junction 11 and follow take the A27 Eastern Way towards Gosport. Turn left at the roundabout to join the A32 Gosport Road and head south into Gosport. Continue along the A32 as it becomes Fareham Road then, at the second roundabout in a junction with two roundabouts, take the 3rd exit (signposted Alverstoke, Stokes Bay, Privett Park) into Military Road. Continue straight down this road, pass the playing fields on the left, then turn left at the roundabout into Privett Road. The entrance to the ground is the 4th turning on the left, just after the junction with Privett Place.

HAVANT & WATERLOOVILLE FC

Founded: 1998
Former Names: Formed by the amalgamation of Waterlooville FC and Havant Town FC
Nickname: 'The Hawks'
Ground: Westleigh Park, Martin Road, Havant, PO9 5TH
Record Attendance: 4,200 (2006/07)
Pitch Size: 112 × 76 yards

Colours: White shirts with Blue shorts
Telephone Nº: (023) 9278-7822 (Ground)
Fax Number: (023) 9226-2367
Ground Capacity: 6,200
Seating Capacity: 665
Web site: www.havantandwaterloovillefc.co.uk

GENERAL INFORMATION

Car Parking: Space for 300 cars at the ground
Coach Parking: At the ground
Nearest Railway Station: Havant (1 mile)
Nearest Bus Station: Town Centre (1½ miles)
Club Shop: At the ground
Opening Times: Matchdays only
Telephone Nº: 07768 271143

GROUND INFORMATION

Away Supporters' Entrances & Sections:
Martin Road End

ADMISSION INFO (2015/2016 PRICES)

Adult Standing: £12.00
Adult Seating: £12.00
Senior Citizen Standing/Seating: £9.00
Concessionary Standing/Seating: £9.00
Note: When accompanied by a paying adult, children under the age of 11 are admitted free of charge

DISABLED INFORMATION

Wheelchairs: 16 spaces available in the Main Stand
Helpers: Admitted
Prices: Normal prices for disabled fans. Free for helpers
Disabled Toilets: Two available
Contact: (023) 9226-7822 (Bookings are necessary)

Travelling Supporters' Information:
Routes: From London or the North take the A27 from Chichester and exit at the B2149 turn-off for Havant. Take the 2nd exit off the dual carriageway into Bartons Road and then the 1st right into Martin Road for the ground; From the West: Take the M27 then the A27 to the Petersfield exit. Then as above.

HAYES & YEADING UNITED FC

Hayes & Yeading United FC are groundsharing with Maidenhead United FC during the 2015/2016 season.

Founded: 2007
Former Names: Formed by the amalgamation of Hayes FC and Yeading FC in 2007
Nickname: 'United'
Ground: York Road, Maidenhead, Berks. SL6 1SF
Pitch Size: 110 × 75 yards

Colours: Red Shirts with Black shorts
Telephone Nº: (020) 8753-2075
Fax Number: (020) 8753-0933
Ground Capacity: 4,500
Seating Capacity: 400
Web site: www.hyufc.com

GENERAL INFORMATION
Car Parking: Street parking
Coach Parking: Street parking
Nearest Railway Station: Maidenhead (¼ mile)
Nearest Bus Station: Maidenhead
Club Shop: None at present
Opening Times: –
Telephone Nº: –

GROUND INFORMATION
Away Supporters' Entrances & Sections:
No usual segregation

ADMISSION INFO (2015/2016 PRICES)
Adult Standing: £12.00   **Adult Seating**: £12.00
Concessionary Standing and Seating: £8.00
Under-18s Standing and Seating: £8.00
Under-16s Standing and Seating: £2.00
Note: Concessionary prices are available for season ticket holders of Premier and Football League clubs as well as those higher in the Non-League pyramid.

DISABLED INFORMATION
Wheelchairs: Accommodated
Helpers: Admitted
Prices: Normal prices for the disabled. Free for helpers
Disabled Toilets: Available
Contact: (01628) 636078   (Bookings are not necessary)

Travelling Supporters' Information:
Routes: Exit M4 at Junction 7 and take the A4 to Maidenhead. Cross the River Thames bridge and turn left at the 2nd roundabout passing through the traffic lights. York Road is first right and the ground is approximately 300 yards along on the left.

HEMEL HEMPSTEAD TOWN FC

Founded: 1885
Former Names: Apsley FC and Hemel Hempstead FC
Nickname: 'The Tudors'
Ground: Vauxhall Road, Adeyfield, Hemel Hempstead HP2 4HW
Record Attendance: 2,254 (vs Gosport Borough during the 2013/14 season)

Pitch Size: 112 × 72 yards
Colours: Shirts and Shorts are Red with White trim
Telephone N°: (01442) 264300
Fax Number: (01442) 264322
Ground Capacity: 3,000
Seating Capacity: 350
Web site: www.hemelfc.com

GENERAL INFORMATION
Car Parking: At the ground
Coach Parking: At the ground
Nearest Railway Station: Hemel Hempstead (1½ miles)
Nearest Bus Station: Hemel Hempstead (¾ mile)
Club Shop: None

GROUND INFORMATION
Away Supporters' Entrances & Sections:
No usual segregation

ADMISSION INFO (2015/2016 PRICES)
Adult Standing: £12.00
Adult Seating: £12.00
Concessionary Standing/Seating: £8.00
Under-18s Standing/Seating: £4.00
Under-12s Standing/Seating: £1.00
Programme Price: £2.00

DISABLED INFORMATION
Wheelchairs: Accommodated
Helpers: Admitted
Prices: Normal prices apply
Disabled Toilets: Available in the Clubhouse
Contact: (01442) 259777

Travelling Supporters' Information:
Routes: Exit the M1 at Junction 8 and go straight ahead at the first roundabout. When approaching the 2nd roundabout move into the right hand lane and, as you continue straight across be ready to turn right almost immediately through a gap in the central reservation. This turn-off is Leverstock Green Road and continue along this to the double mini-roundabout. At this roundabout turn left into Vauxhall Road and the ground is on the right at the next roundabout.

MAIDENHEAD UNITED FC

Founded: 1870
Former Names: None
Nickname: 'Magpies'
Ground: York Road, Maidenhead, Berks. SL6 1SF
Record Attendance: 7,920 (1936)
Pitch Size: 110 × 75 yards
Colours: Black and White striped shirts, Black shorts
Telephone N°: (01628) 636314 (Club)
Contact Number: (01628) 636078
Ground Capacity: 4,500
Seating Capacity: 400
Web: www.maidenheadutd.co.uk

GENERAL INFORMATION
Car Parking: Street parking
Coach Parking: Street parking
Nearest Railway Station: Maidenhead (¼ mile)
Nearest Bus Station: Maidenhead
Club Shop: At the ground
Opening Times: Matchdays only
Telephone N°: (01628) 624739

GROUND INFORMATION
Away Supporters' Entrances & Sections:
No usual segregation

ADMISSION INFO (2015/2016 PRICES)
Adult Standing: £10.00
Adult Seating: £10.00
Concessionary Standing and Seating: £6.00
Under-16s Standing and Seating: £3.00
Note: Junior Magpies (Under-16s) are admitted free to matches in the League.

DISABLED INFORMATION
Wheelchairs: Accommodated
Helpers: Admitted
Prices: Normal prices for the disabled. Free for helpers
Disabled Toilets: Available
Contact: (01628) 636078 (Bookings are not necessary)

Travelling Supporters' Information:
Routes: Exit M4 at Junction 7 and take the A4 to Maidenhead. Cross the River Thames bridge and turn left at the 2nd roundabout passing through the traffic lights. York Road is first right and the ground is approximately 300 yards along on the left.

MAIDSTONE UNITED FC

Founded: 1992 (Reformed)
Former Names: Maidstone Invicta FC
Nickname: 'The Stones'
Ground: Gallagher Stadium, James Whatman Way, Maidstone ME14 1LQ
Record Attendance: 2,305 (27th April 2013)

Colours: Amber shirts with Black shorts
Telephone Nº: (01622) 753817
Ground Capacity: 3,000
Seating Capacity: 818
Web Site: www.maidstoneunited.co.uk

GENERAL INFORMATION

Car Parking: Various Pay & Display Car Parks available near the ground
Coach Parking: Maidstone coach park (1¼ miles) – please contact the club for further information
Nearest Railway Station: Maidstone East (¼ mile)
Club Shop: Available at the ground
Opening Times: Saturday Matchdays 12.30pm to 5.00pm; Tuesday Matchdays 6.15pm to 9.30pm.
Telephone Nº: (01622) 753817

GROUND INFORMATION

Away Supporters' Entrances & Sections:
No usual segregation – use the main turnstiles unless otherwise advertised.

ADMISSION INFO (2015/2016 PRICES)

Adult Standing: £12.00
Adult Seating: £14.00
Senior Citizen/Student Standing: £9.00
Senior Citizen/Student Seating: £11.00
Under-17s Standing: £5.00
Under-17s Seating: £7.00
Under-11s Standing: £1.00
Under-11s Seating: £3.00
Programme Price: £2.50

DISABLED INFORMATION

Wheelchairs: Accommodated
Helpers: Admitted
Prices: Normal prices apply for the disabled. Free for helpers
Disabled Toilets: Available
Contact: (01622) 753817 (Bookings are not necessary)

Travelling Supporters' Information:
Routes: Exit the M20 at Junction 6 or the M2 at Junction 3 and follow the A229 into Maidstone. After entering Maidstone, at the second roundabout (by the White Rabbit pub), take the third exit into James Whatman Way for the stadium.

MARGATE FC

Founded: 1896
Former Names: Thanet United FC
Nickname: 'The Gate'
Ground: Hartsdown Park, Hartsdown Road, Margate   CT9 5QZ
Record Attendance: 14,500 vs Spurs (1973)

Colours: Royal Blue shirts and shorts
Telephone Nº: (01843) 221769
Fax Number: (01843) 221769
Ground Capacity: 2,000
Seating Capacity: 350
Web site: www.margate-fc.co.uk

GENERAL INFORMATION
Car Parking: Street parking
Coach Parking: Available at the ground
Nearest Railway Station: Margate (10 minutes walk)
Club Shop: At the ground
Opening Times: Matchdays only
Telephone Nº: (01843) 225566

GROUND INFORMATION
Away Supporters' Entrances & Sections: Segregation only used for selected fixtures

ADMISSION INFO (2015/2016 PRICES)
Adult Standing: £12.00
Adult Seating: £12.00
Concessionary Standing: £9.00
Concessionary Seating: £9.00
Under-16s Standing: £5.00
Under-16s Seating: £5.00
Note: Under-11s are admitted free with a paying adult.
Programme Price: £2.50

DISABLED INFORMATION
Wheelchairs: Accommodated
Helpers: Admitted
Prices: Concessionary prices apply
Disabled Toilets: Available
Contact: (01843) 221769   (Bookings are necessary)

Travelling Supporters' Information:
Routes: Take the M2/A2 to the A299 then the A28 (Thanet Way) into Margate, turn right opposite the Dog & Duck Pub into Hartsdown Road. Proceed over the crossroads and the ground is on the left.

OXFORD CITY FC

Founded: 1882
Former Names: None
Nickname: 'City'
Ground: Oxford City Stadium, Marsh Lane, Marston, Oxford   OX3 0NQ
Record Attendance: 9,500 (1950)

Colours: Blue & White hooped shirts with Blue shorts
Telephone Nº: (01865) 744493   or   07817 885396
Ground Capacity: 3,000
Seating Capacity: 300
Web Site: www.oxfordcityfc.co.uk
E-mail: ctoxford@btinternet.com

GENERAL INFORMATION
Car Parking: At the ground
Coach Parking: At the ground
Nearest Railway Station: Oxford (3¾ miles)
Club Shop: At the ground
Opening Times: Matchdays only
Telephone Nº: (01865) 744493

GROUND INFORMATION
Away Supporters' Entrances & Sections:
No usual segregation

ADMISSION INFO (2015/2016 PRICES)
Adult Standing: £11.00
Adult Seating: £11.00
Concessionary Standing: £6.00
Concessionary Seating: £6.00
Student Standing: £3.00
Student Seating: £3.00
Under-16s Standing: Free of charge
Under-16s Seating: Free of charge

DISABLED INFORMATION
Wheelchairs: Accommodated
Helpers: Admitted
Prices: Normal prices apply for the disabled and helpers
Disabled Toilets: Available
Contact: (01865) 744493   (Bookings are not necessary)

Travelling Supporters' Information:
Routes: The stadium is located by the side of the A40 Northern Bypass Road next to the Marston flyover junction to the north east of Oxford. Exit the A40 at the Marston junction and head into Marsh Lane (B4150). Take the first turn on the left into the OXSRAD Complex then turn immediately left again to follow the approach road to the stadium in the far corner of the site.

ST. ALBANS CITY FC

Founded: 1908
Former Names: None
Nickname: 'The Saints'
Ground: Clarence Park, York Road, St. Albans, Hertfordshire AL1 4PL
Record Attendance: 9,757 (27th February 1926)
Pitch Size: 110 × 80 yards

Colours: Blue shirts with Yellow trim, Blue shorts
Telephone Nº: (01727) 848914
Fax Number: (01727) 848914
Ground Capacity: 5,007
Seating Capacity: 667
Web site: www.sacfc.co.uk

GENERAL INFORMATION
Car Parking: Street parking
Coach Parking: In Clarence Park
Nearest Railway Station: St. Albans City (200 yds)
Club Shop: At the ground
Opening Times: Matchdays only
Telephone Nº: (01727) 864296

GROUND INFORMATION
Away Supporters' Entrances & Sections:
Hatfield Road End when matches are segregated

ADMISSION INFO (2015/2016 PRICES)
Adult Standing/Seating: £15.00
Concessionary Standing/Seating: £10.00
Under-12s Standing/Seating: £4.00
Note: One child under the age of 12 is admitted free with every paying adult.
Programme Price: £2.50

DISABLED INFORMATION
Wheelchairs: Accommodated
Helpers: One admitted per disabled supporter
Prices: Free for disabled, concessionary prices for helpers
Disabled Toilets: Available in the York Road End
Contact: (01727) 864296 (Bookings are not necessary)

Travelling Supporters' Information:
Routes: Take the M1 or M10 to the A405 North Orbital Road and at the roundabout at the start of the M10, go north on the A5183 (Watling Street). Turn right along St. Stephen's Hill and carry along into St. Albans. Continue up Holywell Hill, go through two sets of traffic lights and at the end of St. Peter's Street, take a right turn at the roundabout into Hatfield Road. Follow over the mini-roundabouts and at the second set of traffic lights turn left into Clarence Road and the ground is on the left. Park in Clarence Road and enter the ground via the Park or in York Road and use the entrance by the footbridge.

SUTTON UNITED FC

Founded: 1898
Former Names: Formed by the amalgamation of Sutton Guild Rovers FC and Sutton Association FC
Nickname: 'U's'
Ground: Borough Sports Ground, Gander Green Lane, Sutton, Surrey SM1 2EY
Record Attendance: 14,000 (1970)

Colours: Shirts are Amber with a Chocolate pin-stripe, Amber shorts
Telephone Nº: (020) 8644-4440
Fax Number: (020) 8644-5120
Ground Capacity: 5,013
Seating Capacity: 765
Web site: www.suttonunited.net

GENERAL INFORMATION
Car Parking: 150 spaces behind the Main Stand
Coach Parking: Space for 1 coach in the car park
Nearest Railway Station: West Sutton (adjacent)
Club Shop: At the ground
Opening Times: Matchdays only
Telephone Nº: (020) 8644-4440

GROUND INFORMATION
Away Supporters' Entrances & Sections:
Collingwood Road entrances and accommodation

ADMISSION INFO (2015/2016 PRICES)
Adult Standing: £12.00
Adult Seating: £13.00
Child Standing: £2.00
Child Seating: £3.00
Senior Citizen Standing: £6.00
Senior Citizen Seating: £7.00

DISABLED INFORMATION
Wheelchairs: 8 spaces are available under cover accommodated on the track perimeter
Helpers: Admitted
Prices: Normal prices apply
Disabled Toilets: Available alongside the Standing Terrace
Contact: (020) 8644-4440 (Bookings are necessary)

Travelling Supporters' Information:
Routes: Exit the M25 at Junction 8 (Reigate Hill) and travel North on the A217 for approximately 8 miles. Cross the A232 then turn right at the traffic lights (past Goose & Granit Public House) into Gander Green Lane. The ground is 300 yards on the left; From London: Gander Green Lane crosses the Sutton bypass 1 mile south of Rose Hill Roundabout. Avoid Sutton Town Centre, especially on Saturdays.

TRURO CITY FC

Founded: 1889
Former Names: None
Nickname: 'White Tigers'
Ground: Treyew Road, Truro   TR1 2TH
Record Attendance: 2,637 (31st March 2007)
Colours: All Red shirts and shorts

Telephone Nº: (01872) 225400
Fax Number: (01872) 225402
Ground Capacity: 3,200
Seating Capacity: 1,600
Web Site: www.trurocityfc.net

GENERAL INFORMATION
Car Parking: At the ground
Coach Parking: At the ground
Nearest Railway Station: Truro (½ mile)
Club Shop: None

GROUND INFORMATION
Away Supporters' Entrances & Sections:
No usual segregation

ADMISSION INFO (2015/2016 PRICES)
Adult Standing: £12.00
Adult Seating: £12.00
Concessionary Standing: £8.00
Concessionary Seating: £8.00
Students and Ages 17-18 Standing: £6.00
Students and Ages 17-18 Seating: £6.00
Under-16s Standing: £3.00 (£1.00 with a paying adult)
Under-16s Seating: £3.00 (£1.00 with a paying adult)

DISABLED INFORMATION
Wheelchairs: Accommodated
Helpers: Admitted
Prices: Normal prices apply for the disabled and helpers
Disabled Toilets: Available
Contact: (01872) 225400   (Bookings are not necessary)

Travelling Supporters' Information:
Routes: From the North or East: Take the A30 to the A390 (from the North) or travel straight on the A390 (from the East) to Truro. Continue on the A390 and pass through Truro. The ground is located just to the South West of Truro on the left hand side of the A390 just before the County Hall;   From the West: Take the A390 to Truro. The ground is on the right hand side of the road shortly after crossing the railway line and passing the County Hall;   From the South: Take the A39 to Truro. At the junction with the A390 turn left onto Green Lane and the ground is on the left hand side of the road after approximately ½ mile.

WEALDSTONE FC

Photo courtesy of Steve Foster/Wealdstone FC

Founded: 1899
Former Names: None
Nickname: 'The Stones' or 'The Royals'
Ground: Grosvenor Vale, Ruislip   HA4 6JQ
Record Attendance: 1,638   (vs Rotherham United)
Colours: Royal Blue shirts with White shorts

Telephone Nº: (01895) 637487
Fax Number: (020) 8907-4421
Ground Capacity: 3,607
Seating Capacity: 329
Web site: www.wealdstone-fc.com

GENERAL INFORMATION
Car Parking: 100 spaces available at the ground
Coach Parking: Available outside the ground
Nearest Mainline Station: West Ruislip (1 mile)
Nearest Tube Station: Ruislip (½ mile)
Club Shop: Yes
Opening Times: Orders through the post only
Telephone Nº: –

GROUND INFORMATION
Away Supporters' Entrances & Sections:
No usual segregation

ADMISSION INFO (2015/2016 PRICES)
Adult Standing: £12.00
Adult Seating: £12.00
Concessionary Standing: £7.00
Concessionary Seating: £7.00
Under-16s Standing/Seating: £2.00
Programme Price: £2.50

DISABLED INFORMATION
Wheelchairs: Accommodated
Helpers: Admitted
Prices: Normal prices apply
Disabled Toilets: Available
Contact: (01895) 637487

Travelling Supporters' Information:
Routes: Exit the M25 at Junction 16 and take the A40 towards Uxbridge. At the Polish War Memorial Junction with the A4180, follow the Ruislip signs (West End Road). After about 1½ miles, turn right into Grosvenor Vale for the ground.

WESTON-SUPER-MARE FC

Founded: 1899
Former Names: Christ Church Old Boys FC
Nickname: 'Seagulls'
Ground: Woodspring Stadium, Winterstoke Road, Weston-super-Mare BS24 9AA
Record Attendance: 2,623 (vs Woking in F.A. Cup)
Pitch Size: 110 × 70 yards

Colours: White shirts with Black shorts
Telephone Nº: (01934) 621618
Fax Number: (01934) 622704
Ground Capacity: 3,071
Seating Capacity: 320
Web site: www.westonsmareafc.co.uk

GENERAL INFORMATION
Car Parking: 140 spaces available at the ground
Coach Parking: At the ground
Nearest Railway Station: Weston-super-Mare (1½ miles)
Nearest Bus Station: Weston-super-Mare (1½ miles)
Club Shop: At the ground
Opening Times: Matchdays only
Telephone Nº: (01934) 621618

GROUND INFORMATION
Away Supporters' Entrances & Sections:
No usual segregation

ADMISSION INFO (2015/2016 PRICES)
Adult Standing/Seating: £10.00
Concessionary Standing/Seating: £7.00
Students and Under-24s Standing/Seating: £7.00
Note: Under-8s are admitted free of charge when accompanied by a paying adult or senior citizen. Under-16s are admitted for £2.00 with a paying adult or senior citizen.

DISABLED INFORMATION
Wheelchairs: Accommodated in a special disabled section
Helpers: Admitted
Prices: Normal prices apply
Disabled Toilets: Two available
Contact: (01934) 621618   (Bookings are not necessary)

Travelling Supporters' Information:
Routes: Exit the M5 at Junction 21 and follow the dual carriageway (A370) to the 4th roundabout (Asda Winterstoke). Turn left, go over the mini-roundabout and continue for 800 yards. The ground is on the right.

WHITEHAWK FC

Founded: 1945
Former Names: Whitehawk & Manor Farm Old Boys
Nickname: 'The Hawks'
Ground: The Enclosed Ground, East Brighton Park, Wilson Avenue, Brighton BN2 5TS
Record Attendance: 2,100 (1988/89 season)

Colours: Red shirts and shorts
Telephone Nº: (01273) 609736
Ground Capacity: 3,000
Seating Capacity: 200
Web Site: www.whitehawkfc.co.uk

GENERAL INFORMATION
Car Parking: At the ground
Coach Parking: At the ground
Nearest Railway Station: London Road (3¼ miles)
Club Shop: None
Opening Times: –
Telephone Nº: –

GROUND INFORMATION
Away Supporters' Entrances & Sections:
No usual segregation

ADMISSION INFO (2015/2016 PRICES)
Adult Standing: £12.00
Adult Seating: £12.00
Concessionary Standing: £7.00
Concessionary Seating: £7.00

DISABLED INFORMATION
Wheelchairs: Accommodated
Helpers: Admitted
Prices: Concessionary prices are charged for the disabled and helpers
Disabled Toilets: None
Contact: (01273) 609736 (Bookings are not necessary)

Travelling Supporters' Information:
Routes: Take the M23/A23 to the junction with the A27 on the outskirts of Brighton then follow the A27 towards Lewes. After passing Sussex University on the left, take the slip road onto the B2123 (signposted Falmer, Rottingdean) and continue for approximately 2 miles before turning right at the traffic lights into Warren Road by the Downs Hotel. Continue for approximately 1 mile then turn left at the traffic lights into Wilson Avenue. After 1¼ miles, turn left at the foot of the hill into East Brighton Park.

Football Conference Premier 2014/2015 Season	AFC Telford United	Aldershot Town	Alfreton Town	Altrincham	Barnet	Braintree Town	Bristol Rovers	Chester	Dartford	Dover Athletic	Eastleigh	FC Halifax Town	Forest Green Rovers	Gateshead	Grimsby Town	Kidderminster Harriers	Lincoln City	Macclesfield Town	Nuneaton Town	Southport	Torquay United	Welling United	Woking	Wrexham
AFC Telford United		0-2	0-1	2-1	2-2	1-3	0-1	1-2	2-3	1-4	3-4	0-1	0-1	0-1	1-1	1-1	1-0	2-3	0-0	3-3	4-3	1-2	1-3	1-2
Aldershot Town	1-2		2-0	3-1	1-3	1-3	2-2	0-1	1-1	3-1	0-2	1-1	1-1	1-2	2-1	0-1	1-0	0-1	1-0	1-2	2-0	2-1	0-1	1-1
Alfreton Town	3-2	2-3		1-1	1-1	0-2	0-0	1-1	0-0	2-3	3-2	0-2	2-2	1-2	0-2	2-0	0-0	1-5	1-0	4-2	4-2	2-2	1-3	2-3
Altrincham	1-2	1-0	0-1		1-3	1-0	2-1	4-1	2-1	2-2	3-3	0-0	2-2	0-1	1-1	2-1	1-2	1-0	0-1	2-0	2-1	0-4	0-3	1-4
Barnet	3-1	1-0	2-1	5-0		3-0	2-0	3-0	4-0	2-2	1-0	3-0	1-3	2-0	1-3	3-3	1-2	3-1	1-0	4-0	2-3	5-0	2-1	0-1
Braintree Town	0-2	1-1	2-1	4-2	1-1		2-0	1-3	3-0	3-0	1-5	0-0	1-2	1-0	0-1	2-0	1-3	1-2	2-0	0-2	2-0	0-1	0-0	1-0
Bristol Rovers	1-0	3-1	7-0	1-0	2-1	2-1		5-1	1-0	1-1	1-2	2-1	0-1	3-2	0-0	1-1	2-0	4-0	3-1	2-0	1-1	2-0	2-0	1-0
Chester	2-0	1-0	2-1	0-2	0-5	2-3	2-2		1-2	3-1	0-1	0-3	1-4	1-0	2-2	1-0	4-0	1-0	5-3	0-2	1-1	2-3	2-1
Dartford	2-1	1-1	0-1	1-2	0-1	0-2	2-2	2-4		2-1	2-2	1-2	1-1	1-1	1-2	0-0	1-1	3-1	1-1	0-0	2-1	1-3	1-2
Dover Athletic	1-0	3-0	1-0	2-1	0-3	1-0	1-1	2-0	6-1		2-1	0-1	0-0	1-0	0-1	0-1	1-2	0-1	5-0	2-2	2-2	4-0	2-1	2-0
Eastleigh	3-3	1-0	3-1	0-2	1-2	1-0	1-1	3-2	2-0	0-1		4-1	2-2	2-2	0-1	2-1	1-0	4-0	2-1	2-1	1-2	3-1	2-2	2-2
FC Halifax Town	5-0	1-0	2-0	1-3	1-1	1-0	2-2	0-2	0-0	3-2	0-2		1-0	2-2	1-1	2-0	3-2	2-0	3-1	0-2	3-0	1-3	2-2
Forest Green Rovers	3-0	1-3	2-0	1-1	1-2	1-1	1-1	2-1	2-1	0-0	1-1	2-0		1-1	2-1	2-3	3-3	3-1	1-0	5-3	2-1	4-1	2-1	0-1
Gateshead	4-1	1-1	2-0	1-0	0-2	3-1	0-1	2-1	1-0	1-2	2-3	2-2	2-4		1-6	2-0	3-3	2-1	1-2	1-1	3-1	1-1	0-0	3-1
Grimsby Town	1-0	3-1	7-0	0-0	3-1	1-0	0-1	3-0	1-1	2-1	1-0	2-1	2-2		0-2	1-3	1-2	0-0	1-0	0-2	2-0	3-1	0-1
Kidderminster Harriers	1-1	0-2	3-0	4-0	1-1	3-1	0-3	2-2	1-0	2-4	2-1	0-1		2-1	0-2	3-1	0-1	2-1	2-1	1-1	1-1
Lincoln City	2-0	3-0	3-2	1-2	4-1	3-2	2-3	0-1	1-0	1-2	1-1	1-2	1-1	3-2	0-0		2-0	3-1	1-0	1-3	0-2	0-2	1-1
Macclesfield Town	1-0	0-0	2-0	2-1	2-1	1-0	0-0	3-1	2-0	1-0	2-0	1-2	1-1	0-1	0-0	3-0		0-1	3-0	1-0	3-2	2-1	2-2
Nuneaton Town	4-4	1-1	0-1	2-1	0-2	0-1	0-2	3-2	1-2	3-2	1-3	1-2	1-0	0-2	0-2	2-1	1-1		2-3	0-0	1-0	1-1	0-2
Southport	0-3	1-3	0-2	2-1	0-2	0-2	0-1	0-0	2-0	2-2	1-2	1-0	0-1	2-2	1-0	3-3	1-1	0-0		2-1	1-0	2-5	0-1
Torquay United	0-1	1-1	1-1	2-0	1-2	1-5	1-2	0-1	1-1	2-0	2-0	2-1	3-3	2-2	2-3	2-1	1-0	1-1	4-0	0-0		3-0	1-0	2-1
Welling United	1-1	3-1	2-3	0-1	1-2	2-1	0-0	1-3	2-2	0-2	1-2	1-1	1-1	0-2	3-0	0-0	4-1	0-1	0-0		1-1	2-1
Woking	1-3	1-2	3-0	2-0	1-1	1-0	0-1	1-1	6-1	1-1	3-2	1-0	3-0	1-2	2-3	3-1	1-0	1-2	3-2	2-2		1-1
Wrexham	0-4	3-1	4-0	2-3	1-0	3-0	0-0	1-0	1-3	1-1	3-0	0-0	0-0	0-3	0-1	1-0	1-1	2-2	1-0	0-0	0-0	2-1	1-2	

Football Conference National

Season 2014/2015

Barnet	46	28	8	10	94	46	92
Bristol Rovers	46	25	16	5	73	34	91
Grimsby Town	46	25	11	10	74	40	86
Eastleigh	46	24	10	12	87	61	82
Forest Green Rovers	46	22	16	8	80	54	79
Macclesfield Town	46	21	15	10	60	46	78
Woking	46	21	13	12	77	52	76
Dover Athletic	46	19	11	16	69	68	68
Halifax Town	46	17	15	14	60	54	66
Gateshead	46	17	15	14	66	62	66
Wrexham	46	17	15	14	56	52	66
Chester	46	19	6	21	64	76	63
Torquay United	46	16	13	17	64	60	61
Braintree Town	46	18	5	23	56	57	59
Lincoln City	46	16	10	20	62	71	58
Kidderminster Harriers	46	15	12	19	51	60	57
Altrincham	46	16	8	22	54	73	56
Aldershot Town	46	14	11	21	51	61	53
Southport	46	13	12	21	47	72	51
Welling United	46	11	12	23	52	73	45
Alfreton Town	46	12	9	25	49	90	45
AFC Telford United	46	10	9	27	58	84	39
Dartford	46	8	15	23	44	74	39
Nuneaton Town	46	10	9	27	38	76	36

Forest Green Rovers had 3 points deducted for fielding an ineligible player.

Nuneaton Town had 3 points deducted for fielding an ineligible player.

Promotion Play-offs

Forest Green Rovers 0   Bristol Rovers 1
Eastleigh 1   Grimsby Town 2

Bristol Rovers 2   Forest Green Rovers 0
Bristol Rovers won 3-0 on aggregate.

Grimsby Town 3   Eastleigh 0
Grimsby Town won 5-1 on aggregate.

Bristol Rovers 1   Grimsby Town .... 1 (aet)
Bristol Rovers won 5-3 on penalties.

Promoted: Barnet and Bristol Rovers

Relegated: Alfreton Town, AFC Telford United, Dartford and Nuneaton Town

	AFC Fylde	Barrow	Boston United	Brackley Town	Bradford Park Avenue	Chorley	Colwyn Bay	Gainsborough Trinity	Gloucester City	Guiseley	Harrogate Town	Hednesford Town	Hyde	Leamington	Lowestoft Town	North Ferriby United	Oxford City	Solihull Moors	Stalybridge Celtic	Stockport County	Tamworth	Worcester City
AFC Fylde	■	3-2	3-0	4-0	2-1	1-3	6-2	2-1	6-4	0-0	1-2	3-1	1-1	3-1	3-1	1-0	2-1	2-2	3-0	0-0	1-1	4-0
Barrow	1-2	■	1-0	3-1	0-0	4-0	3-1	3-1	5-0	1-0	1-1	2-1	3-1	2-1	2-0	4-1	2-2	1-3	1-0	1-0	4-1	1-0
Boston United	3-1	2-1	■	1-1	5-0	0-0	5-0	2-1	2-0	5-1	5-2	0-2	3-1	0-0	5-3	0-1	2-7	1-2	1-1	1-1	2-0	2-0
Brackley Town	0-2	1-0	0-1	■	2-1	0-1	1-1	3-2	1-0	0-3	1-0	1-0	1-0	2-1	2-3	1-1	0-5	0-1	1-0	0-1	0-0	0-0
Bradford Park Avenue	0-1	2-1	1-3	0-0	■	3-2	2-2	1-2	1-1	0-0	2-1	1-0	3-2	2-1	1-1	1-1	0-5	2-3	1-0	2-0	2-4	0-1
Chorley	2-2	0-0	1-2	2-1	2-1	■	0-0	4-1	1-2	1-0	4-0	2-0	3-2	2-2	2-2	1-0	1-1	0-0	2-0	3-0	6-0	3-3
Colwyn Bay	0-5	0-1	2-3	1-0	0-0	0-2	■	4-1	3-1	1-3	0-1	0-3	3-3	1-5	0-1	0-0	3-5	1-4	0-1	1-2	2-0	0-2
Gainsborough Trinity	0-0	0-2	1-1	1-2	1-0	3-4	6-3	■	2-2	1-2	0-1	1-0	3-3	1-0	0-0	3-0	1-2	3-1	2-1	2-0	1-1	1-2
Gloucester City	0-2	2-0	0-1	2-1	3-3	2-1	1-1	0-1	■	1-3	1-0	0-0	1-1	3-1	2-0	1-1	1-7	1-1	0-1	2-1	1-2	2-0
Guiseley	3-1	2-3	2-0	3-1	1-2	2-1	1-1	1-3	1-4	■	4-2	0-2	2-0	1-0	2-0	2-3	4-0	3-0	0-2	3-0	2-2	1-0
Harrogate Town	1-4	2-2	2-1	5-0	0-2	4-1	0-2	0-0	2-1	0-0	■	0-2	4-1	1-1	1-1	4-1	1-0	0-4	1-0	2-1	0-0	0-3
Hednesford Town	2-0	1-1	1-2	4-1	1-1	2-1	0-2	2-1	3-1	1-1	3-2	■	4-1	1-2	2-0	1-2	0-2	1-1	1-2	1-1	2-3	0-0
Hyde	1-1	4-4	1-3	1-2	1-3	3-3	2-4	1-2	2-4	0-0	1-1	0-1	■	2-2	5-1	1-0	0-1	1-0	2-4	1-1	2-2	0-3
Leamington	1-4	0-2	1-1	2-1	4-3	1-3	0-3	2-1	4-1	0-1	1-3	1-1	4-0	■	1-2	2-2	4-0	1-0	1-1	0-2	1-2	2-2
Lowestoft Town	1-0	2-3	1-1	0-1	3-2	3-1	1-1	2-0	0-3	0-0	0-0	2-2	3-0	1-1	■	1-2	2-1	2-0	1-1	2-2	3-2	1-1
North Ferriby United	1-1	2-2	2-0	1-1	0-0	3-4	2-4	2-1	2-2	4-4	1-0	0-2	3-0	3-1	1-2	■	4-3	1-3	2-0	1-1	0-0	3-0
Oxford City	1-8	0-3	0-0	2-1	1-2	0-0	3-1	2-0	2-2	4-2	1-1	0-3	2-0	3-1	2-1	1-1	■	1-4	1-2	2-1	1-0	0-0
Solihull Moors	0-1	3-4	1-4	1-0	4-1	3-1	0-0	2-0	0-2	0-1	1-1	3-0	2-0	3-3	2-4	2-3	■	1-2	2-2	0-2	1-4	
Stalybridge Celtic	3-0	0-1	1-1	1-5	0-1	0-1	1-2	4-4	2-1	1-3	2-1	0-5	7-1	0-1	1-1	2-2	0-2	0-3	■	3-2	3-1	0-1
Stockport County	0-0	0-1	3-2	2-1	3-1	0-2	1-1	1-3	5-3	0-3	2-1	3-0	2-0	4-2	3-0	0-1	1-2	1-0	4-3	■	0-2	2-0
Tamworth	0-3	1-1	1-1	2-1	2-0	0-3	1-1	0-1	2-1	1-0	3-0	3-1	5-0	3-2	2-0	2-2	4-3	3-1	4-1	0-1	■	1-0
Worcester City	0-4	0-2	1-1	1-1	0-1	2-0	3-5	2-0	1-2	1-1	2-0	2-2	4-1	2-1	2-1	2-1	1-0	1-4	2-2	2-0	1-1	■

Football Conference North

Season 2014/2015

Barrow	42	26	9	7	81	43	87
AFC Fylde	42	25	10	7	93	43	85
Boston United	42	20	12	10	75	51	72
Chorley	42	20	11	11	76	55	71
Guiseley	42	20	10	12	68	49	70
Oxford City	42	20	9	13	81	67	69
Tamworth	42	19	12	11	66	57	69
Hednesford Town	42	17	10	15	63	50	61
Worcester City	42	16	12	14	54	54	60
North Ferriby United	42	14	16	12	65	63	58
Stockport County	42	16	9	17	56	59	57
Solihull Moors	42	16	7	19	68	63	55
Bradford Park Avenue	42	14	11	17	52	66	53
Gloucester City	42	14	10	18	63	75	52
Harrogate Town	42	14	10	18	50	62	52
Lowestoft Town	42	12	15	15	54	66	51
Gainsborough Trinity	42	14	8	20	59	67	50
Brackley Town	42	13	8	21	39	62	47
Stalybridge Celtic	42	12	9	21	54	70	45
Colwyn Bay	42	11	12	19	59	82	45
Leamington	42	10	10	22	59	74	40
Hyde	42	3	12	27	49	106	21

Promotion Play-offs North

Guiseley .... 1 AFC Fylde 0
Chorley .... 0 Boston United 0

AFC Fylde .... 1 Guiseley 2
Guiseley won 3-1 on aggregate.
Boston United .... 2 Chorley .... 2 (aet)
Aggregate 2-2. Chorley won 5-4 on penalties.

Chorley .... 2 Guiseley 3

Promoted: Barrow and Guiseley
Relegated: Colwyn Bay, Leamington and Hyde

Football Conference South 2014/2015 Season

	Basingstoke Town	Bath City	Bishop's Stortford	Boreham Wood	Bromley	Chelmsford	Concord Rangers	Eastbourne Borough	Ebbsfleet United	Farnborough	Gosport Borough	Havant & Waterlooville	Hayes & Yeading United	Hemel Hempstead Town	Maidenhead United	St. Albans City	Staines Town	Sutton United	Wealdstone	Weston-super-Mare	Whitehawk
Basingstoke Town	■	3-2	0-1	2-1	1-2	1-2	0-0	1-0	1-0	3-1	1-1	0-0	2-0	0-1	3-2	0-1	2-1	2-2	2-4	2-1	1-0
Bath City	0-4	■	0-1	2-0	2-2	0-0	1-1	2-0	2-1	7-4	1-3	1-2	0-0	1-0	4-0	2-0	2-1	0-2	0-1	3-0	1-4
Bishop's Stortford	2-3	1-1	■	0-5	1-1	2-3	3-1	1-1	1-1	2-2	0-1	0-2	2-2	1-3	1-3	2-1	2-1	0-0	2-2	3-4	3-1
Boreham Wood	0-4	1-2	2-0	■	1-1	4-0	0-0	5-2	1-3	2-0	1-1	1-2	3-0	1-0	2-1	2-1	3-0	2-0	2-1	4-0	2-2
Bromley	0-3	1-0	3-2	2-1	■	0-1	1-2	2-1	1-2	5-0	0-3	2-0	1-1	0-1	4-2	1-0	0-1	2-1	1-1	3-0	4-1
Chelmsford City	1-1	2-1	4-2	3-4	1-2	■	0-1	3-2	1-5	6-2	0-1	0-1	1-1	4-0	1-1	2-1	1-3	1-1	0-2	3-2	2-1
Concord Rangers	2-3	3-0	3-3	1-1	1-4	2-1	■	1-3	1-0	7-0	0-0	3-2	0-1	0-1	2-2	3-1	1-0	0-0	4-2	2-0	3-0
Eastbourne Borough	3-0	0-1	3-0	4-1	1-4	2-0	1-0	■	1-1	0-0	1-0	1-3	2-1	0-2	2-2	1-0	4-2	1-0	1-1	3-1	2-2
Ebbsfleet United	1-5	0-0	4-0	1-1	0-1	0-2	2-0	0-0	■	3-0	0-3	1-0	1-2	2-2	1-0	4-1	3-2	3-0	0-0	0-1	3-0
Farnborough	2-1	2-7	0-1	0-3	1-2	1-3	0-3	2-1	0-3	■	1-4	0-5	1-0	2-2	1-1	0-1	1-1	0-1	1-4	2-3	2-0
Gosport Borough	0-0	3-1	2-0	0-1	2-1	0-1	1-1	1-1	2-2	2-1	■	3-1	4-0	1-1	1-2	2-1	3-2	0-0	1-1	1-2	
Havant & Waterlooville	2-0	2-0	0-1	2-1	1-3	2-3	0-1	2-1	2-0	1-0	3-2	■	4-2	2-0	1-0	0-0	3-1	2-2	3-1	1-0	1-2
Hayes & Yeading United	0-1	2-0	2-1	0-3	1-2	2-1	3-1	0-1	0-2	2-0	2-3	0-1	■	2-4	1-1	0-3	0-0	1-1	2-1	1-2	0-1
Hemel Hempstead Town	4-3	0-3	0-3	0-6	1-1	3-1	1-2	0-0	1-1	4-1	2-1	1-1	1-1	■	1-1	3-1	5-1	1-2	1-1	1-1	0-2
Maidenhead United	0-3	1-1	1-3	0-1	4-4	2-0	1-2	0-0	0-4	0-1	1-2	0-2	2-0	0-2	■	1-1	2-0	2-1	1-4	6-2	0-2
St. Albans City	1-1	1-0	2-1	0-2	2-2	0-2	2-0	3-0	1-0	2-3	2-1	1-0	0-1	1-1	4-1	■	0-0	2-4	1-3	2-0	2-3
Staines Town	0-3	1-1	1-0	2-1	0-6	3-5	0-2	0-1	0-2	1-2	2-1	1-2	2-3	0-4	1-2	2-3	■	0-1	1-2	0-1	1-2
Sutton United	2-1	1-3	2-2	1-3	1-2	1-0	1-1	1-1	2-1	2-0	0-1	1-0	0-1	1-2	1-2	2-1	4-2	■	1-1	1-2	0-2
Wealdstone	0-1	1-2	1-4	0-1	0-4	4-2	1-0	1-1	0-1	1-2	3-0	2-2	0-2	2-2	1-1	0-3	1-0	1-1	■	1-3	0-2
Weston-super-Mare	1-2	4-2	0-1	1-4	0-1	3-1	1-2	2-2	3-2	4-3	0-5	2-1	2-2	1-6	0-2	0-2	1-2	3-2	1-2	■	1-1
Whitehawk	0-1	2-1	1-0	3-0	2-1	5-1	1-1	2-0	1-0	1-1	1-0	0-0	2-0	3-1	3-4	2-1	1-2	0-2	0-1	2-1	■

Football Conference South
Season 2014/2015

Bromley	40	23	8	9	79	46	77
Boreham Wood	40	23	6	11	79	44	75
Basingstoke Town	40	22	7	11	67	43	73
Whitehawk	40	22	6	12	62	47	72
Havant & Waterlooville	40	21	7	12	61	41	70
Gosport Borough	40	19	10	11	63	40	67
Concord Rangers	40	18	11	11	60	44	65
Ebbsfleet United	40	17	9	14	60	41	60
Hemel Hempstead Town	40	16	12	12	64	60	60
Chelmsford City	40	17	5	18	65	71	56
Eastbourne Borough	40	14	13	13	51	50	55
Wealdstone	40	14	12	14	56	56	54
St Albans City	40	16	6	18	53	53	54
Bath City	40	15	8	17	59	57	53
Sutton United	40	13	11	16	50	54	50
Bishop's Stortford	40	12	10	18	55	69	46
Weston-super-Mare	40	13	5	22	55	86	44
Maidenhead United	40	10	13	17	54	70	43
Hayes & Yeading United	40	11	9	20	39	58	42
Farnborough	40	8	6	26	42	101	30
Staines Town	40	7	4	29	39	82	25

Promotion Play-offs South

Havant & Waterlooville 0   Boreham Wood 2
Whitehawk 1   Basingstoke Town 1

Boreham Wood 2   Havant & Waterlooville 2
Boreham Wood won 4-2 on aggregate.
Basingstoke Town 0   Whitehawk 1
Whitehawk won 2-1 on aggregate.

Boreham Wood 2   Whitehawk .... 1 (aet)

Promoted: Bromley and Boreham Wood
Relegated: Farnborough and Staines Town

Northern Premier League Premier Division 2014/2015 Season

	Ashton United	Barwell	Belper Town	Blyth Spartans	Buxton	Curzon Ashton	FC United of Manchester	Frickley Athletic	Grantham Town	Halesowen Town	Ilkeston	King's Lynn Town	Marine	Matlock Town	Nantwich Town	Ramsbottom United	Rushall Olympic	Skelmersdale United	Stamford	Stourbridge	Trafford	Whitby Town	Witton Albion	Workington
Ashton United	■	3-1	4-3	3-0	1-1	2-2	0-2	2-2	2-0	1-0	0-2	3-1	2-2	2-0	3-1	1-0	1-2	1-0	0-1	3-0	1-1	1-0	2-1	3-2
Barwell	1-0	■	1-0	2-1	1-2	1-1	0-0	2-2	3-0	0-1	2-1	4-3	2-1	1-3	3-2	3-4	3-1	2-0	1-0	2-2	2-0	1-0	0-2	1-2
Belper Town	2-2	2-2	■	3-4	1-1	2-0	1-3	2-0	1-2	2-1	2-3	3-3	2-2	3-3	1-4	1-2	0-3	1-1	2-3	0-4	2-0	0-2	5-0	1-2
Blyth Spartans	1-1	1-1	2-0	■	0-1	2-1	0-1	1-1	2-1	2-1	0-1	3-2	1-2	0-0	2-1	4-0	3-3	1-1	4-1	2-0	1-0	2-2	2-1	1-0
Buxton	2-3	1-1	5-1	2-3	■	2-1	1-1	4-0	5-1	2-1	1-1	1-1	1-1	3-2	0-1	1-1	0-3	1-2	1-2	4-1	3-2	1-1	0-3	1-1
Curzon Ashton	3-2	4-1	2-2	1-1	0-0	■	0-4	3-0	2-4	4-1	4-0	4-0	1-0	3-0	0-1	1-0	2-3	2-0	3-1	2-1	3-0	2-1	3-0	0-0
FC United of Manchester	3-0	3-1	2-2	0-0	1-1	1-1	■	3-2	3-1	1-0	2-2	3-1	5-2	0-0	2-1	3-1	1-0	1-2	3-1	1-0	3-0	2-1	4-0	1-0
Frickley Athletic	1-3	1-3	2-0	2-1	1-1	1-1	4-1	■	2-4	1-1	0-2	1-1	1-0	1-0	0-1	4-2	1-1	0-1	0-2	1-0	4-0	1-1	2-3	1-2
Grantham Town	0-0	1-1	1-0	1-7	3-1	1-1	1-2	1-1	■	0-2	1-0	3-3	1-1	2-1	4-0	0-1	0-1	1-1	1-4	1-1	4-3	0-1	3-1	1-1
Halesowen Town	2-3	4-1	1-1	1-2	2-1	0-0	0-1	1-1	1-1	■	0-0	1-1	1-0	4-3	1-1	2-0	3-0	2-0	1-1	2-0	1-1	3-3	1-0	0-1
Ilkeston	0-0	2-1	1-0	1-1	0-0	1-1	3-1	1-0	1-1	2-2	■	3-3	1-0	2-1	2-4	2-1	2-0	1-2	3-4	6-0	1-1	1-1	0-3
King's Lynn Town	1-1	0-1	1-0	1-3	1-2	1-3	1-2	2-1	1-0	0-0	3-0	■	3-1	1-3	2-1	2-1	0-4	0-3	1-0	1-0	0-1	0-1	2-0	1-2
Marine	1-0	2-0	2-2	3-3	1-2	1-1	0-0	2-0	2-2	1-1	1-2	1-2	■	0-2	0-1	1-3	2-1	1-0	2-0	1-1	2-2	2-1	0-1	0-1
Matlock Town	0-1	3-1	3-1	1-1	0-0	0-3	0-0	3-0	0-2	0-4	0-0	3-1	3-2	■	2-1	1-1	1-2	1-2	4-1	2-4	1-3	3-0	0-1
Nantwich Town	1-3	2-0	2-1	1-1	1-1	1-2	1-2	3-2	0-3	1-0	1-1	2-1	2-1	3-0	■	3-2	0-1	0-1	0-3	2-3	0-0	2-1	3-0	2-3
Ramsbottom United	0-3	0-1	4-2	3-3	2-0	1-1	0-2	0-0	3-1	1-1	1-2	2-3	3-2	0-1	1-4	■	2-3	0-3	3-1	0-1	1-2	4-0	3-2	1-1
Rushall Olympic	1-2	0-3	2-1	1-2	3-0	2-1	1-1	1-3	0-0	1-1	1-3	2-3	1-1	1-0	2-1	2-4	■	0-0	0-0	3-0	6-1	1-5	2-1	3-0
Skelmersdale United	1-1	1-3	2-1	1-0	2-3	1-1	1-0	3-2	1-1	1-4	1-1	3-1	0-1	1-0	3-0	1-2	■	0-3	2-1	3-0	4-0	1-0	1-0
Stamford	0-2	0-2	0-1	1-1	1-3	0-1	1-1	1-3	1-1	1-2	0-4	2-1	0-1	0-1	2-2	1-1	3-0	1-3	■	2-3	3-3	1-1	3-2	2-1
Stourbridge	1-1	0-2	4-0	0-3	0-3	2-1	2-1	1-2	1-1	3-3	3-0	2-2	1-0	5-3	1-2	0-0	1-1	■	1-1	2-1	3-0	0-1
Trafford	1-2	1-1	2-2	1-4	0-1	1-1	2-3	3-1	0-2	2-4	1-3	2-3	0-0	4-0	0-1	0-3	0-1	2-2	2-2	■	3-3	1-1	2-3
Whitby Town	2-0	0-1	3-3	1-0	0-1	0-1	0-4	1-1	2-1	0-0	1-3	2-2	2-2	1-1	3-1	2-0	2-1	0-2	3-0	1-0	1-1	■	1-1	0-0
Witton Albion	5-2	2-2	0-0	1-5	1-1	1-3	0-0	1-2	1-3	2-0	1-4	0-1	3-1	1-3	3-0	2-1	3-2	2-0	3-0	2-1	0-5	0-3	■	1-2
Workington	1-2	2-1	3-0	1-1	1-2	3-2	1-0	1-1	2-2	1-0	0-0	2-0	2-0	0-1	0-0	1-0	3-2	1-2	1-0	1-0	3-0	1-2	■

Evo-Stik League – Northern Premier Division
Season 2014/2015

FC United of Manchester	46	26	14	6	78	37	92
Workington	46	27	9	10	63	39	90
Ashton United	46	24	12	10	75	54	84
Curzon Ashton	46	23	14	9	79	46	83
Ilkeston	46	22	15	9	79	56	81
Blyth Spartans	46	21	16	9	84	54	79
Skelmersdale United	46	21	10	15	58	48	73
Barwell	46	21	10	15	69	63	73
Rushall Olympic	46	21	9	16	76	64	72
Buxton	46	18	17	11	70	57	71
Halesowen Town	46	13	20	13	56	48	59
Grantham Town	46	15	14	17	64	72	59
Whitby Town	46	14	16	16	56	63	58
Matlock Town	46	15	11	20	57	60	56
Nantwich Town	46	16	7	23	61	76	55
Stourbridge	46	14	11	21	59	72	53
Ramsbottom United	46	15	8	23	66	80	53
King's Lynn Town	46	14	10	22	60	81	52
Frickley Athletic	46	12	14	20	60	73	50
Stamford	46	13	11	22	56	75	50
Marine	46	11	16	19	58	69	49
Witton Albion	46	14	7	25	58	86	49
Trafford	46	6	15	25	58	93	33
Belper Town	46	6	14	26	62	96	32

Promotion Play-offs

Workington 0   Ilkeston 1
Ashton United 1   Curzon Ashton .... 1 (aet)
Curzon Ashton won 4-2 on penalties.

Curzon Ashton 1   Ilkeston 0

Promoted: FC United of Manchester and Curzon Ashton
Relegated: Witton Albion, Trafford and Belper Town

Southern Football League Premier Division 2014/2015 Season	Arlesey Town	Banbury United	Bideford	Biggleswade Town	Burnham	Cambridge City	Chesham United	Chippenham Town	Cirencester Town	Corby Town	Dorchester Town	Dunstable Town	Frome Town	Histon	Hitchin Town	Hungerford Town	Paulton Rovers	Poole Town	Redditch United	Slough Town	St. Neots Town	Truro City	Weymouth
Arlesey Town		2-2	0-1	2-1	2-1	0-2	0-3	0-0	1-2	1-2	1-0	0-2	2-2	2-1	0-2	2-3	0-0	0-2	1-3	1-0	1-3	2-3	0-1
Banbury United	0-2		2-3	2-2	0-2	2-0	1-1	2-4	0-5	0-5	2-1	2-1	1-1	4-0	0-3	1-2	0-1	0-1	0-0	3-0	1-1	1-2	3-0
Bideford	3-0	2-2		0-1	4-2	1-1	1-3	5-0	0-2	1-3	1-0	1-2	4-0	2-0	2-1	1-0	3-0	0-6	1-1	2-0	1-1	1-3	1-2
Biggleswade Town	0-1	0-0	3-0		1-0	1-4	1-3	0-2	1-0	3-2	4-1	0-2	1-2	1-1	3-7	1-1	1-0	1-2	2-5	3-3	2-2	3-2	4-2
Burnham	0-4	0-3	5-1	1-1		1-2	0-2	0-0	0-1	0-3	1-5	2-0	3-1	1-3	0-0	2-2	2-3	1-3	0-2	0-2	0-1	2-2	1-2
Cambridge City	1-1	6-1	1-0	1-1	3-0		1-0	1-1	1-3	2-2	3-0	1-2	2-2	6-0	2-4	2-1	1-0	0-2	0-2	3-3	0-0	1-1	0-1
Chesham United	1-3	1-0	4-2	3-2	2-0	4-4		0-3	0-3	0-1	3-2	1-3	3-0	2-1	0-1	1-2	2-2	1-3	0-1	0-0	3-3	3-0	7-2
Chippenham Town	3-0	3-0	1-1	1-1	3-1	1-1	1-1		2-1	0-2	2-1	1-0	1-0	1-0	2-3	0-1	1-1	1-0	1-2	2-0	0-1	1-2	2-3
Cirencester Town	1-1	1-5	6-2	1-1	1-0	4-0	2-2	1-1		0-0	6-1	1-1	3-1	2-0	2-3	1-1	0-1	3-2	3-2	3-5	1-1	2-0	0-3
Corby Town	3-2	2-1	1-2	2-0	3-1	3-1	1-1	2-1	2-1		2-2	2-2	3-0	1-0	2-0	1-1	4-1	1-0	0-0	1-2	1-3	1-0	5-1
Dorchester Town	3-1	3-1	3-3	0-1	1-0	2-2	0-0	0-1	0-1	2-1		1-2	1-1	2-0	1-0	3-4	2-1	0-1	3-1	1-1	1-2	2-0	0-3
Dunstable Town	5-1	2-3	1-1	1-0	4-2	1-1	3-2	5-1	0-3	1-2	3-5		0-4	1-3	2-6	0-2	2-1	2-4	1-3	1-2	1-3
Frome Town	2-3	4-2	0-2	1-2	1-2	2-1	1-1	0-0	0-1	1-2	1-3	0-1		4-2	0-3	1-0	2-0	0-1	0-4	1-1	1-1	1-0	3-1
Histon	1-0	3-0	1-2	3-0	2-1	1-1	6-5	1-3	1-1	1-2	1-0	1-0	1-2		1-1	2-1	2-1	1-1	1-1	0-0	0-0	3-1	3-0
Hitchin Town	2-0	2-0	3-2	1-0	4-0	2-1	4-1	1-1	0-0	2-4	0-0	3-2	1-1	0-0		0-2	1-0	4-0	5-2	3-4	1-2	0-3
Hungerford Town	2-0	4-0	2-0	1-1	1-0	2-0	2-0	0-0	1-1	3-0	0-2	0-0	1-1	1-0	2-1		2-1	0-0	1-1	2-0	0-0	2-0	2-0
Paulton Rovers	6-2	0-0	2-1	3-2	3-0	1-1	1-1	2-1	2-1	1-0	1-2	2-2	1-0	0-3	3-0	2-3		4-5	1-0	2-2	0-0	1-2	1-0
Poole Town	3-1	2-0	1-2	1-0	1-0	3-2	3-0	3-1	2-1	2-3	0-0	1-0	7-0	2-0	2-2	1-0	1-0		0-1	2-1	0-0	3-0	4-0
Redditch United	2-0	1-1	7-2	1-0	0-0	2-4	2-2	2-1	0-0	0-1	3-0	2-0	2-0	0-0	0-2	0-2	0-1		4-0	2-0	0-4	1-1
Slough Town	1-0	2-1	4-1	1-1	2-2	0-4	0-3	2-2	1-2	1-2	2-1	0-3	1-1	1-1	2-1	1-2	4-2	0-4	1-7		3-3	1-2	3-0
St Neots Town	3-0	2-1	1-0	2-1	3-1	0-1	2-3	3-0	4-0	2-4	6-5	3-3	3-1	4-0	6-2	1-1	1-1	3-2	0-3	0-3		0-2	2-0
Truro City	3-1	4-1	5-0	2-1	2-1	1-0	0-3	2-0	1-4	2-1	1-0	2-1	7-2	3-0	2-1	2-0	2-2	3-2	1-2	2-2		2-0
Weymouth	3-0	3-2	2-1	3-2	3-3	1-0	2-1	0-1	2-0	0-1	2-0	2-2	4-2	3-0	2-2	3-1	2-4	0-0	1-1	3-2	1-0	1-1	

Evo-Stik Southern Premier
Premier Division

Season 2014/2015

Corby Town	44	29	7	8	86	47	94
Poole Town	44	28	7	9	84	35	91
Truro City	44	27	5	12	83	58	86
Hungerford Town	44	22	13	9	64	36	79
St. Neots Town	44	20	16	8	82	58	76
Redditch United	44	21	12	11	73	44	75
Weymouth	44	22	7	15	71	71	73
Cirencester Town	44	20	12	12	77	54	72
Hitchin Town	44	20	10	14	78	63	70
Paulton Rovers	44	18	10	16	65	62	64
Chippenham Town	44	16	13	15	54	54	61
Chesham United	44	16	12	16	79	72	60
Cambridge City	44	14	15	15	71	62	57
Dunstable Town	44	16	9	19	71	78	57
Bideford	44	16	7	21	66	85	55
Slough Town	44	13	12	19	66	88	51
Dorchester Town	44	14	8	22	63	74	50
Histon	44	13	10	21	53	74	49
Biggleswade Town	44	11	12	21	57	75	45
Frome Town	44	10	11	23	49	80	41
Banbury United	44	9	10	25	53	86	37
Arlesey Town	44	10	6	28	43	84	36
Burnham	44	5	8	31	41	89	20

Burnham had 3 points deducted for fielding an ineligible player.
Hereford United FC was liquidated on 19th December 2014 and the club's record was expunged on 5th January 2015.

Promotion Play-offs

Poole Town 0   St. Neots Town 1
Truro City 1   Hungerford Town 0

Truro City 1   St. Neots Town 0

Promoted: Corby Town and Truro City
Relegated: Banbury United, Arseley Town and Burnham

Ryman League Premier Division 2014/2015 Season

	AFC Hornchurch	Billericay Town	Bognor Regis Town	Bury Town	Canvey Island	Dulwich Hamlet	East Thurrock United	Enfield Town	Grays Athletic	Hampton & Richmond Borough	Harrow Borough	Hendon	Kingstonian	Leatherhead	Leiston	Lewes	Maidstone United	Margate	Metropolitan Police	Peacehaven & Telscombe	Tonbridge Angels	VCD Athletic	Wingate & Finchley	Witham Town
AFC Hornchurch		2-2	0-0	1-1	2-0	1-0	1-1	0-1	2-0	0-1	1-3	0-2	0-0	1-3	1-1	0-1	0-2	0-2	2-2	1-1	0-0	2-0	0-1	2-1
Billericay Town	3-1		1-2	4-1	0-1	2-1	2-0	5-0	2-0	1-1	0-1	0-2	0-2	2-0	4-0	2-2	1-3	4-3	3-0	1-1	3-3	2-1	2-3	3-0
Bognor Regis Town	1-2	1-1		1-1	2-1	4-0	0-1	2-1	1-2	3-0	2-0	4-1	1-1	1-2	2-2	1-2	3-4	0-1	2-0	3-1	0-0	2-1	3-2	5-2
Bury Town	1-4	2-1	1-1		1-0	1-3	0-1	1-1	0-2	2-1	1-3	0-3	1-1	0-0	0-2	1-2	1-4	2-1	1-2	2-1	2-3	1-2	0-0	
Canvey Island	0-3	1-0	3-1	3-4		1-2	1-2	2-1	1-1	0-4	0-1	1-3	1-1	1-3	1-1	1-2	2-2	4-4	2-1	5-2	1-0	3-2	1-1	
Dulwich Hamlet	2-0	2-1	0-1	3-0	0-3		3-3	2-1	2-0	2-2	3-2	0-0	2-1	4-1	1-2	2-0	0-0	2-1	0-0	3-1	2-0	1-2	3-3	1-0
East Thurrock United	1-0	2-1	1-1	1-1	1-0	2-2		1-1	0-2	1-0	1-3	1-1	0-1	1-1	1-0	0-0	1-1	1-1	0-5	4-0	2-1	3-2	0-0	2-1
Enfield Town	3-2	4-0	2-0	1-0	3-2	0-1	0-2		2-2	1-0	5-0	1-0	2-5	3-1	0-2	3-0	0-4	3-1	1-0	1-0	2-1	1-0	2-3	1-2
Grays Athletic	1-0	2-0	0-1	2-0	1-2	1-0	1-3	3-1		3-2	2-1	0-0	3-1	1-1	1-1	1-3	0-0	0-2	0-1	3-1	1-1	3-2	4-0	
Hampton & Richmond Borough	2-1	1-2	1-1	1-0	1-2	1-0	2-1	1-0	0-4		2-1	2-2	2-0	1-5	4-6	2-1	2-1	2-0	2-2	1-3	0-1	2-1	1-4	2-4
Harrow Borough	0-3	1-2	1-2	3-1	1-0	1-3	2-4	2-0	1-4	1-2		2-2	2-0	3-2	2-0	1-1	1-1	2-2	2-0	1-1	2-0	2-0	5-1	3-3
Hendon	4-2	1-1	1-0	2-0	2-2	1-1	0-3	3-2	2-2	2-0			2-0	2-1	1-2	3-2	2-1	3-2	1-1	3-1	1-1			
Kingstonian	1-0	2-2	1-2	0-0	1-1	1-1	2-2	0-1	0-2	1-1	0-1	2-2		2-2	0-1	3-0	0-1	3-3	3-1	3-0	1-0	0-1	3-2	1-1
Leatherhead	2-1	0-1	4-3	4-0	1-0	2-0	2-1	0-2	3-1	3-1	1-2	2-3	1-2		1-0	1-1	1-0	1-1	2-2	1-2	0-1	2-0	1-2	
Leiston	4-0	2-1	3-2	0-1	1-1	0-2	1-2	2-2	3-0	2-0	0-0	0-1	1-2			3-0	2-2	0-1	1-1	5-0	2-1	1-2	2-0	1-1
Lewes	2-2	0-2	1-0	1-0	1-2	1-0	3-2	2-1	3-2	0-0	0-1	1-2	1-0	0-1	0-2		0-2	1-5	2-0	2-2	0-0	2-2	3-0	1-2
Maidstone United	2-0	3-0	2-1	1-0	5-2	1-1	3-2	0-3	2-1	2-0	2-1	1-1	4-1	2-1	4-1	2-1		2-1	3-1	2-0	1-1	2-0	3-0	1-1
Margate	5-1	5-1	3-1	3-0	4-2	1-2	3-1	0-3	3-0	1-0	3-3	4-4	2-0	1-0	1-1	3-0	1-0		2-1	1-2	2-2	0-3	0-0	2-1
Metropolitan Police	2-1	2-1	2-0	4-1	1-1	0-0	5-0	1-0	3-0	1-2	2-0	2-0	3-3	3-1	2-0	2-0	0-3		2-0	2-1	1-0	1-2	3-1	
Peacehaven & Telscombe	2-1	0-2	1-1	1-0	0-1	0-1	4-3	0-2	2-5	2-4	4-1	2-0	1-2	2-5	0-4	1-1	0-2	2-0		4-1	1-1	1-2	3-3	
Tonbridge Angels	4-0	0-1	1-1	1-1	4-1	2-2	3-1	2-1	1-2	2-0	1-1	3-3	0-2	0-3	1-2	2-0	1-0	2-2	0-2	1-2		4-1	1-2	3-0
VCD Athletic	0-2	2-0	1-3	1-1	2-2	0-3	2-2	2-1	1-2	3-2	1-3	1-1	2-0	2-2	0-2	0-3	1-1	0-2	0-3	1-1			2-0	
Wingate & Finchley	1-0	0-1	4-1	4-0	2-0	3-0	3-4	1-0	1-0	2-2	3-1	1-2	1-2	0-0	3-4	2-0	0-2	1-1	0-2	1-1	2-0	2-0		3-2
Witham Town	2-1	2-3	2-2	4-1	1-1	0-0	2-0	1-2	1-1	3-2	3-1	1-2	2-3	2-3	1-1	1-1	1-3	1-2	0-2	1-0	2-2	1-1	1-0	

Ryman League Premier Division

Season 2014/2015

Maidstone United	46	29	11	6	85	41	98
Hendon	46	27	14	5	82	55	95
Margate	46	25	10	11	94	58	85
Dulwich Hamlet	46	21	13	12	66	51	76
Metropolitan Police	46	21	12	13	72	51	75
Grays Athletic	46	22	8	16	70	57	74
Enfield Town	46	24	4	18	70	56	73
Billericay Town	46	20	8	18	73	65	68
Leiston	46	18	13	15	73	58	67
Leatherhead	46	19	10	17	72	62	67
Kingstonian	46	18	13	15	63	56	67
Wingate & Finchley	46	20	7	19	72	70	67
East Thurrock United	46	17	15	14	66	71	66
Bognor Regis Town	46	17	12	17	71	64	63
Hampton & Richmond	46	16	9	21	62	79	57
Harrow Borough	46	15	8	23	64	77	53
Canvey Island	46	14	11	21	61	77	53
VCD Athletic	46	14	11	21	53	70	53
Lewes	46	14	11	21	45	67	53
Tonbridge Angels	46	13	13	20	63	67	52
Peacehaven & Telscombe	46	13	9	24	58	85	48
Witham Town	46	9	15	22	61	84	42
AFC Hornchurch	46	10	10	26	46	70	40
Bury Town	46	7	11	28	35	86	32

Enfield Town had 3 points deducted for fielding an ineligible player.

Promotion Play-offs

Hendon 2   Metropolitan Police 1
Margate 2   Dulwich Hamlet 1

Hendon 0   Margate 1

Promoted: Maidstone United and Margate

Relegated: Peacehave & Telscombe, Witham Town, AFC Hornchurch and Cray Wanderers

81

F.A. Trophy 2014/2015

Qualifying 1	Skelmersdale United	0	Nantwich Town	2
Qualifying 1	Sheffield	0	Witton Albion	1
Qualifying 1	New Mills	3	Mossley	2
Qualifying 1	Prescot Cables	2	Goole	4
Qualifying 1	Farsley	0	Blyth Spartans	2
Qualifying 1	Whitby Town	1	Ramsbottom United	2
Qualifying 1	FC United Of Manchester	2	Padiham	0
Qualifying 1	Frickley Athletic	0	Marine	2
Qualifying 1	Scarborough Athletic	0	Darlington 1883	4
Qualifying 1	Curzon Ashton	0	Northwich Victoria	0
Qualifying 1	Buxton	2	Ashton United	0
Qualifying 1	Clitheroe	0	Workington	2
Qualifying 1	Ossett Town	2	Trafford	2
Qualifying 1	Spennymoor Town	3	Bamber Bridge	1
Qualifying 1	St. Neots Town	2	Ilkeston	1
Qualifying 1	Mickleover Sports	3	Kettering Town	2
Qualifying 1	Carlton Town	1	Stourbridge	1
Qualifying 1	Corby Town	0	Redditch United	1
Qualifying 1	Loughborough Dynamo	3	Grantham Town	1
Qualifying 1	Belper Town	2	Histon	3
Qualifying 1	Halesowen Town	1	Matlock Town	1
Qualifying 1	Evesham United	2	Banbury United	2
Qualifying 1	Gresley	3	Romulus	1
Qualifying 1	Stamford	0	Barwell	1
Qualifying 1	Chasetown	2	Newcastle Town	1
Qualifying 1	Rushall Olympic	2	Cambridge City	0
Qualifying 1	Market Drayton Town	2	King's Lynn Town	2
Qualifying 1	Stratford Town	1	Stafford Rangers	0
Qualifying 1	Leek Town	2	Spalding United	2
Qualifying 1	Aylesbury	1	Merstham	2
Qualifying 1	Walton Casuals	2	Peacehaven & Telscombe	4
Qualifying 1	Dulwich Hamlet	3	Chalfont St. Peter	0
Qualifying 1	Thamesmead Town	3	Three Bridges	1
Qualifying 1	Metropolitan Police	1	Billericay Town	0
Qualifying 1	Whyteleafe	3	Dunstable Town	1
Qualifying 1	Maidstone United	3	Walton & Hersham	2
Qualifying 1	Bedford Town	4	Brightlingsea Regent	0
Qualifying 1	Worthing	1	Chatham Town	1
Qualifying 1	Horsham	1	Ware	0
Qualifying 1	Canvey Island	1	Leatherhead	1
Qualifying 1	Folkestone Invicta	3	Thurrock	2
Qualifying 1	Margate	0	Slough Town	2
Qualifying 1	Arlesey Town	2	Wingate & Finchley	1
Qualifying 1	Uxbridge	6	Hythe Town	1
Qualifying 1	Brentwood Town	1	Biggleswade Town	1
Qualifying 1	Hampton & Richmond Borough	0	Grays Athletic	3
Qualifying 1	Burgess Hill Town	2	Chesham United	0
Qualifying 1	Northwood	2	Guernsey	2 (aet)
	Northwood won 5-3 on penalties			
Qualifying 1	Lewes	1	Harlow Town	0
Qualifying 1	Cray Wanderers	3	Faversham Town	0
Qualifying 1	VCD Athletic	0	Tonbridge Angels	2
Qualifying 1	Hungerford Town	1	East Thurrock United	1
Qualifying 1	Dereham Town	1	Enfield Town	0
Qualifying 1	Bognor Regis Town	2	AFC Sudbury	2

Qualifying 1	Bury Town	1	Hendon	3	
Qualifying 1	Royston Town	1	Witham Town	2	
Qualifying 1	Burnham	2	Hitchin Town	2	
Qualifying 1	Barkingside	3	Kingstonian	1	
Qualifying 1	South Park	1	Heybridge Swifts	4	
Qualifying 1	Leiston	2	Leighton Town	2	
Qualifying 1	AFC Hornchurch	2	Harrow Borough	0	
Qualifying 1	Mangotsfield United	5	Bishop's Cleeve	1	
Qualifying 1	Sholing	1	Tiverton Town	0	
Qualifying 1	AFC Totton	1	Hereford United	2	
Qualifying 1	Truro City	3	Egham Town	0	
Qualifying 1	Poole Town	3	North Leigh	1	
Qualifying 1	Paulton Rovers	3	Fleet Town	0	
Qualifying 1	Chippenham Town	3	Frome Town	1	
Qualifying 1	Merthyr Town	2	Cirencester Town	0	
Qualifying 1	Weymouth	1	Shortwood United	0	
Qualifying 1	Dorchester Town	1	Wimborne Town	3	
Qualifying 1	Bideford	3	Didcot Town	3	
Replay	Northwich Victoria	0	Curzon Ashton	1	
Replay	Trafford	3	Ossett Town	0	
Replay	Stourbridge	4	Carlton Town	2	
Replay	Matlock Town	0	Halesowen Town	4	
Replay	Banbury United	1	Evesham United	0	
Replay	King's Lynn Town	5	Market Drayton Town	1	
Replay	Spalding United	1	Leek Town	2	
Replay	Chatham Town	0	Worthing	1	
Replay	Leatherhead	2	Canvey Island	2	(aet)
	Leatherhead won 6-5 on penalties				
Replay	Biggleswade Town	3	Brentwood Town	2	
Replay	East Thurrock United	4	Hungerford Town	2	
Replay	AFC Sudbury	2	Bognor Regis Town	1	
Replay	Hitchin Town	0	Burnham	2	
Replay	Leighton Town	2	Leiston	5	
Replay	Didcot Town	2	Bideford	1	
Qualifying 2	Chasetown	4	Loughborough Dynamo	1	
Qualifying 2	Spennymoor Town	3	Leek Town	3	
Qualifying 2	Rushall Olympic	5	Stratford Town	0	
Qualifying 2	Blyth Spartans	1	Halesowen Town	1	
Qualifying 2	St. Neots Town	3	Darlington 1883	1	
Qualifying 2	Curzon Ashton	1	Barwell	2	
Qualifying 2	Witton Albion	3	Workington	3	
Qualifying 2	King's Lynn Town	3	Stourbridge	1	
Qualifying 2	Redditch United	5	Trafford	2	
Qualifying 2	Gresley	2	Goole	0	
Qualifying 2	FC United of Manchester	2	Buxton	0	
Qualifying 2	Nantwich Town	1	Ramsbottom United	3	
Qualifying 2	Mickleover Sports	3	New Mills	1	
Qualifying 2	Banbury United	3	Marine	2	
Qualifying 2	Hereford United	2	Mangotsfield United	0	
Qualifying 2	Witham Town	0	Truro City	1	
Qualifying 2	Dereham Town	0	Sholing	2	
Qualifying 2	Weymouth	0	Burnham	0	
Qualifying 2	Maidstone United	0	AFC Sudbury	2	
Qualifying 2	Metropolitan Police	2	Dulwich Hamlet	0	
Qualifying 2	Barkingside	1	Horsham	3	
Qualifying 2	Peacehaven & Telscombe	4	Thamesmead Town	3	
Qualifying 2	Lewes	1	Heybridge Swifts	1	

Round	Home	Score	Away	Score	Notes
Qualifying 2	Leiston	3	Paulton Rovers	2	
Qualifying 2	Burgess Hill Town	0	Folkestone Invicta	0	
Qualifying 2	Slough Town	1	Merthyr Town	1	
Qualifying 2	Biggleswade Town	1	Poole Town	2	
Qualifying 2	Uxbridge	1	Didcot Town	2	
Qualifying 2	Bedford Town	2	Chippenham Town	1	
Qualifying 2	Whyteleafe	1	Leatherhead	4	
Qualifying 2	AFC Hornchurch	4	Merstham	2	
Qualifying 2	Histon	0	Cray Wanderers	2	
Qualifying 2	East Thurrock United	4	Arlesey Town	4	
Qualifying 2	Hendon	4	Worthing	0	
Qualifying 2	Tonbridge Angels	2	Grays Athletic	0	
Qualifying 2	Wimborne Town	2	Northwood	1	
Replay	Leek Town	0	Spennymoor Town	1	
Replay	Halesowen Town	2	Blyth Spartans	0	
Replay	Workington	3	Witton Albion	0	
Replay	Burnham	0	Weymouth	0	(aet)
	Weymouth won 5-4 on penalties				
Replay	Heybridge Swifts	2	Lewes	3	
Replay	Folkestone Invicta	0	Burgess Hill Town	1	
Replay	Merthyr Town	3	Slough Town	2	
Replay	Arlesey Town	1	East Thurrock United	2	
Qualifying 3	Boston United	2	Workington	1	
Qualifying 3	AFC Fylde	3	Hednesford Town	2	
Qualifying 3	Gainsborough Trinity	2	Brackley Town	1	
Qualifying 3	Stockport County	2	Colwyn Bay	1	
Qualifying 3	Bradford (Park Avenue)	3	Leamington	1	
Qualifying 3	King's Lynn Town	0	Harrogate Town	1	
Qualifying 3	Halesowen Town	2	Gresley	0	
Qualifying 3	Worcester City	3	Barrow	0	
Qualifying 3	Chorley	2	Stalybridge Celtic	2	
Qualifying 3	Tamworth	3	Hyde	4	
Qualifying 3	North Ferriby United	6	Mickleover Sports	2	
Qualifying 3	Spennymoor Town	3	Chasetown	0	
Qualifying 3	Barwell	1	FC United of Manchester	1	
Qualifying 3	Solihull Moors	2	Redditch United	1	
Qualifying 3	Guiseley	0	Rushall Olympic	0	
Qualifying 3	Banbury United	0	Ramsbottom United	3	
Qualifying 3	Sholing	1	Farnborough	2	
Qualifying 3	Concord Rangers	4	Boreham Wood	0	
Qualifying 3	Weymouth	3	Cray Wanderers	1	
Qualifying 3	Merthyr Town	3	Didcot Town	3	
Qualifying 3	Bedford Town	0	Weston Super Mare	0	
Qualifying 3	Hayes & Yeading United	6	Horsham	0	
Qualifying 3	Oxford City	6	Lewes	1	
Qualifying 3	Truro City	1	Hemel Hempstead Town	2	
Qualifying 3	Tonbridge Angels	0	Bromley	0	
Qualifying 3	Bishop's Stortford	4	Chelmsford City	3	
Qualifying 3	Eastbourne Borough	1	Lowestoft Town	2	
Qualifying 3	St. Neots Town	1	AFC Sudbury	1	
Qualifying 3	Ebbsfleet United	1	Hendon	0	
Qualifying 3	Maidenhead United	1	Metropolitan Police	0	
Qualifying 3	Basingstoke Town	1	Whitehawk	0	
Qualifying 3	Havant & Waterlooville	2	East Thurrock United	1	
Qualifying 3	Peacehaven & Telscombe	0	Gosport Borough	4	
Qualifying 3	Wimborne Town	4	AFC Hornchurch	2	
Qualifying 3	St. Albans City	1	Wealdstone	1	

Qualifying 3	Gloucester City	0	Bath City	0	
Qualifying 3	Staines Town	3	Poole Town	3	
Qualifying 3	Burgess Hill Town	3	Leatherhead	2	
Qualifying 3	Hereford United	1	Sutton United	2	
Qualifying 3	Leiston received a bye and progressed to the next round.				
Replay	Stalybridge Celtic	1	Chorley	2	
Replay	FC United of Manchester	3	Barwell	2	
Replay	Rushall Olympic	1	Guiseley	2	
Replay	Didcot Town	2	Merthyr Town	1	
Replay	Weston Super Mare	3	Bedford Town	2	(aet)
Replay	Bromley	3	Tonbridge Angels	0	
Replay	AFC Sudbury	1	St. Neots Town	0	
Replay	Wealdstone	3	St. Albans City	0	
Replay	Bath City	3	Gloucester City	1	(aet)
Replay	Poole Town	1	Staines Town	1	(aet)
	Poole Town won 5-4 on penalties				
Round 1	Nuneaton Town	0	Grimsby Town	2	
Round 1	Hyde	4	Spennymoor Town	2	
Round 1	Altrincham	1	Macclesfield Town	0	
Round 1	AFC Fylde	3	Gainsborough Trinity	0	
Round 1	Guiseley	0	Chorley	2	
Round 1	Lincoln City	0	Alfreton Town	2	
Round 1	North Ferriby United	1	Boston United	1	
Round 1	Gateshead	2	Halesowen Town	0	
Round 1	Worcester City	0	FC Halifax Town	1	
Round 1	Southport	1	Wrexham	1	
Round 1	Ramsbottom United	0	Stockport County	3	
Round 1	Bradford (Park Avenue)	1	Kidderminster Harriers	4	
Round 1	AFC Telford United	1	Chester	1	
Round 1	FC United Of Manchester	4	Harrogate Town	0	
Round 1	Aldershot Town	0	Burgess Hill Town	1	
Round 1	Weymouth	1	Havant & Waterlooville	1	
Round 1	Bishop's Stortford	0	Torquay United	5	
Round 1	Lowestoft Town	1	Dover Athletic	3	
Round 1	Ebbsfleet United	1	Welling United	1	
Round 1	Wealdstone	1	Hayes & Yeading United	0	
Round 1	Wimborne Town	0	Oxford City	3	
Round 1	Weston Super Mare	1	Farnborough	3	
Round 1	Dartford	2	Solihull Moors	0	
Round 1	Woking	2	Eastleigh	0	
Round 1	Hemel Hempstead Town	1	Sutton United	0	
Round 1	Basingstoke Town	2	Gosport Borough	2	
Round 1	Bromley	2	Leiston	0	
Round 1	Forest Green Rovers	2	Didcot Town	2	
Round 1	Bristol Rovers	0	Bath City	2	
Round 1	Maidenhead United	2	Poole Town	1	
Round 1	Braintree Town	1	AFC Sudbury	0	
Round 1	Concord Rangers	0	Barnet	0	
Replay	Boston united	0	North Ferriby United	2	
Replay	Wrexham	2	Southport	0	
Replay	Chester	1	AFC Telford United	1	(aet)
	AFC Telford United won 4-3 on penalties.				
Replay	Havant & Waterlooville	5	Weymouth	0	
Replay	Welling United	2	Ebbsfleet United	3	(aet)
Replay	Gosport Borough	2	Basingstoke Town	1	(aet)
Replay	Didcot Town	0	Forest Green Rovers	3	

85

Replay	Barnet	2	Concord Rangers	6	
Round 2	Chorley	3	FC United Of Manchester	3	
Round 2	Grimsby Town	0	Gateshead	0	
Round 2	Stockport County	2	Wrexham	2	
Round 2	FC Halifax Town	5	Alfreton Town	3	
Round 2	North Ferriby United	2	Hyde	0	
Round 2	AFC Fylde	4	AFC Telford United	0	
Round 2	Kidderminster Harriers	0	Altrincham	1	
Round 2	Wealdstone	1	Bath City	3	
Round 2	Ebbsfleet United	1	Forest Green Rovers	0	
Round 2	Havant & Waterlooville	0	Dover Athletic	1	
Round 2	Maidenhead United	2	Farnborough	2	
Round 2	Gosport Borough	0	Braintree Town	2	
Round 2	Oxford City	2	Woking	2	
Round 2	Hemel Hempstead Town	3	Concord Rangers	1	
Round 2	Torquay United	4	Bromley	0	
Round 2	Burgess Hill Town	1	Dartford	2	
Replay	FC United Of Manchester	1	Chorley	0	
Replay	Gateshead	3	Grimsby Town	2	(aet)
Replay	Wrexham	6	Stockport County	1	
Replay	Farnborough	1	Maidenhead United	0	
Replay	Woking	2	Oxford City	1	
Round 3	Wrexham	1	Gateshead	1	
Round 3	Braintree Town	1	Ebbsfleet United	1	
Round 3	FC United Of Manchester	3	AFC Fylde	1	
Round 3	Dartford	2	FC Halifax Town	2	
Round 3	Farnborough	0	North Ferriby United	2	
Round 3	Hemel Hempstead Town	0	Torquay United	2	
Round 3	Bath City	1	Altrincham	0	
Round 3	Woking	3	Dover Athletic	3	
Replay	Gateshead	2	Wrexham	2	(aet)
	Wrexham won 5-3 on penalties.				
Replay	Ebbsfleet United	2	Braintree Town	0	
Replay	FC Halifax Town	3	Dartford	1	
Replay	Dover Athletic	1	Woking	0	
Round 4	Dover Athletic	3	Bath City	3	
Round 4	FC Halifax Town	0	Wrexham	1	
Round 4	Torquay United	1	FC United of Manchester	0	
Round 4	North Ferriby United	1	Ebbsfleet United	0	
Replay	Bath City	2	Dover Athletic	1	
Semi-finals					
1st leg	Bath City	2	North Ferriby United	2	
2nd leg	North Ferriby United	1	Bath City	1	(aet)
	Aggregate 3-3. North Ferriby United won 4-2 on penalties.				
Semi-final	Wrexham	2	Torquay United	1	
Semi-final	Torquay United	0	Wrexham	3	
	Wrexham won 5-1 on aggregate.				
FINAL	North Ferriby United	3	Wrexham	3	(aet)
	North Ferriby United won 5-4 on penalties.				

F.A. Vase 2014/2015

Round 1	Colne	2	Shildon	3	(aet)
Round 1	Bootle	2	Barton Town OBs	5	
Round 1	Dronfield Town	2	Chadderton	1	
	Chadderton progressed to the next round after Dronfield Town were disqualified from the competition.				
Round 1	West Allotment Celtic	2	Runcorn Town	4	
Round 1	North Shields	4	AFC Emley	2	
Round 1	Daisy Hill	0	Atherton Collieries	8	
Round 1	1874 Northwich	2	Ashton Town	1	
Round 1	Marske United	5	Winterton Rangers	0	
Round 1	Bishop Auckland	3	Holker Old Boys	0	
Round 1	Bottesford Town	1	Ryhope CW	1	(aet)
Round 1	Selby Town	2	Seaham Red Star	4	
Round 1	Guisborough Town	3	Billingham Synthonia	1	
Round 1	Shaw Lane Aquaforce	4	Runcorn Linnets	1	
Round 1	St. Helens Town	3	Yorkshire Amateur	1	
Round 1	Sunderland RCA	1	Handsworth Parramore	0	
Round 1	Bedlington Terriers	1	Whitley Bay	4	
Round 1	AFC Darwen	2	Maine Road	0	
Round 1	Winsford United	2	Tadcaster Albion	3	
Round 1	Consett	2	Silsden	1	
Round 1	West Didsbury & Chorlton	1	Glossop North End	2	
Round 1	Gedling MW	0	AFC Mansfield	2	
Round 1	Long Eaton United	0	Worksop Town	3	
Round 1	Walsall Wood	3	AFC Bridgnorth	2	
Round 1	Borrowash Victoria	2	Belper United	1	(aet)
Round 1	Pegasus Juniors	4	Aston	0	
Round 1	Boldmere St. Michaels	2	Thurnby Nirvana	4	
Round 1	Rocester	3	Brocton	6	
Round 1	Bromsgrove Sporting	3	Nuneaton Griff	2	
Round 1	Ellistown & Ibstock United	2	Hanley Town	1	(aet)
Round 1	Blidworth Welfare	0	Willenhall Town	2	
Round 1	Southam United	1	Cleethorpes Town	5	
Round 1	Shepshed Dynamo	5	Oadby Town	0	
Round 1	Mickleover Royals	3	Eccleshall	0	
Round 1	Dunkirk	7	Graham St. Prims	2	
Round 1	Gornal Athletic	3	Studley	2	
Round 1	AFC Wulfrunians	0	Heanor Town	0	(aet)
Round 1	Wellington	2	Bolehall Swifts	3	
Round 1	Welwyn Garden City	1	Peterborough Sports	2	(aet)
Round 1	Eton Manor	0	St. Margaretsbury	1	
Round 1	Deeping Rangers	1	Wivenhoe Town	0	
Round 1	Woodbridge Town	0	Huntingdon Town	3	
Round 1	Irchester United	0	Fakenham Town	4	
Round 1	Oxhey Jets	4	Tower Hamlets	1	
Round 1	Kirkley & Pakefield	2	Colney Heath	3	
	Kirkley & Pakefield progressed to the next round after Colney Heath were disqualified.				
Round 1	Saffron Walden Town	2	Whitton United	1	
Round 1	Hertford Town	1	Stanway Rovers	1	(aet)
	Stanway Rovers won 6-5 on penalties				
Round 1	Holbeach United	2	Gorleston	0	
Round 1	Sun Sports	3	Harefield United	1	
Round 1	Haringey Borough	1	Northampton Spencer	1	(aet)
Round 1	Berkhamsted	0	Kings Langley	3	
Round 1	Peterborough Northern Star	1	Stotfold	0	
Round 1	AFC Kempston Rovers	3	Felixstowe & Walton United	1	

Round 1	Ipswich Wanderers	1	Cockfosters	0	
Round 1	AFC Dunstable	5	Haverhill Borough	2	
Round 1	Enfield 1893	0	Tring Athletic	4	
Round 1	Godmanchester Rovers	0	Yaxley	0	(aet)
Round 1	Waltham Forest	1	Great Yarmouth Town	2	
Round 1	Wembley	3	Bowers & Pitsea	2	
Round 1	London Colney	2	Baldock Town	1	
Round 1	Colliers Wood United	4	Ringmer	3	(aet)
Round 1	Chessington & Hook United	2	Camberley Town	1	(aet)
Round 1	Eastbourne Town	1	Erith & Belvedere	2	(aet)
Round 1	Hassocks	3	Corinthian	1	
Round 1	Littlehampton Town	4	Guildford City	2	(aet)
Round 1	Ashford Town (Middx)	2	Loxwood	3	
Round 1	Fisher	2	Crawley Down Gatwick	2	(aet)
Round 1	Lingfield	5	Epsom & Ewell	1	
Round 1	Horsham YMCA	3	Bedfont Sports	1	
Round 1	Raynes Park Vale	1	Westfield	3	
Round 1	Chertsey Town	1	Horley Town	2	
Round 1	Arundel	0	Phoenix Sports	2	
Round 1	Lordswood	0	Knaphill	1	
Round 1	Greenwich Borough	7	Hailsham Town	1	
Round 1	Tunbridge Wells	3	Rochester United	1	
Round 1	Erith Town	4	Banstead Athletic	1	
Round 1	Pagham	2	Spelthorne Sports	1	
Round 1	Thatcham Town	1	Flackwell Heath	4	
Round 1	Bradford Town	5	Malmesbury Victoria	3	
Round 1	Ardley United	1	Chippenham Park	2	
Round 1	Hook Norton	0	Newport (IW)	2	
Round 1	Ringwood Town	1	United Services Portsmouth	3	
Round 1	Windsor	1	Highworth Town	4	
Round 1	Holmer Green	2	Ascot United	2	(aet)
Round 1	Verwood Town	2	Fareham Town	0	
Round 1	Calne Town	1	Bridport	2	(aet)
Round 1	Melksham Town	2	Highmoor Ibis	1	(aet)
Round 1	Thame United	2	Chinnor	1	
Round 1	Bemerton Heath Harlequins	2	Cowes Sports	0	
Round 1	Winchester City	0	Horndean	3	
Round 1	Farnham Town	3	Abingdon United	3	(aet)
Round 1	AFC Portchester	2	Reading Town	1	
Round 1	Folland Sports	2	Sherborne Town	1	
Round 1	AFC St. Austell	4	Saltash United	0	
Round 1	Plymouth Parkway	4	Tuffley Rovers	1	
Round 1	Buckland Athletic	1	Longwell Green Sports	0	(aet)
Round 1	St. Blazey	4	Gillingham Town	1	
Round 1	Shepton Mallet	2	Brislington	1	
Round 1	Welton Rovers	3	Brimscombe & Thrupp	1	
Round 1	Newquay	1	Slimbridge	3	
Round 1	Odd Down	4	Falmouth Town	3	
Round 1	Bristol Manor Farm	3	Radstock Town	0	
Round 1	Alnwick Town	80	Bye	0	
Replay	Ryhope CW	2	Bottesford Town	1	
Replay	Heanor Town	3	AFC Wulfrunians	0	
Replay	Northampton Spencer	0	Haringey Borough	0	(aet)
	Northampton Spencer won 4-3 on penalties				
Replay	Yaxley	4	Godmanchester Rovers	0	
Replay	Crawley Down Gatwick	2	Fisher	2	(aet)
	Crawley Down Gatwick won 4-3 on penalties				

88

Replay	Ascot United	7	Holmer Green	0	
Replay	Abingdon united	5	Farnham Town	1	
Round 2	Bishop Auckland	1	1874 Northwich	4	
Round 2	Glossop North End	3	Ryhope CW	0	
Round 2	Alnwick Town	4	St. Helens Town	5	(aet)
Round 2	Dunston UTS	2	Guisborough Town	1	
Round 2	Newcastle Benfield	2	Ashington	1	
Round 2	Marske United	4	Barton Town Old Boys	1	
Round 2	West Auckland Town	0	Shaw Lane Aquaforce	3	
Round 2	AFC Darwen	3	Chadderton	5	
Round 2	Shildon	2	Runcorn Town	0	
Round 2	Sunderland RCA	0	North Shields	3	
Round 2	Atherton Collieries	1	Seaham Red Star	2	
Round 2	Congleton Town	0	Whitley Bay	1	
Round 2	Consett	8	Whickham	0	
Round 2	Tadcaster Albion	2	Morpeth Town	1	
Round 2	Worksop Town	2	Ellistown & Ibstock United	1	
Round 2	Bolehall Swifts	4	Dunkirk	2	
Round 2	Westfields	2	St. Andrews	1	
Round 2	Wisbech Town	2	Cleethorpes Town	1	
Round 2	Thurnby Nirvana	4	Gornal Athletic	1	
Round 2	Shepshed Dynamo	2	AFC Mansfield	3	(aet)
Round 2	Heanor Town	4	Coleshill Town	3	
Round 2	Borrowash Victoria	0	Bromsgrove Sporting	5	
Round 2	Mickleover Royals	2	Willenhall Town	0	
Round 2	Brocton	3	Pegasus Juniors	1	
Round 2	Causeway United	1	Walsall Wood	5	
Round 2	Sun Sports	0	Stanway Rovers	1	
Round 2	London Colney	3	Northampton Spencer	1	
Round 2	St. Margaretsbury	3	Ipswich Wanderers	0	
Round 2	Peterborough Sports	3	Peterborough NS	4	
Round 2	Hullbridge Sports	1	AFC Rushden & Diamonds	0	
Round 2	Holbeach United	3	Huntingdon Town	2	
Round 2	Norwich United	2	AFC Kempston Rovers	1	
Round 2	Yaxley	3	Fakenham Town	0	
Round 2	Deeping Rangers	2	Oxhey Jets	0	
Round 2	AFC Dunstable	3	Kirkley & Pakefield	2	
Round 2	Saffron Walden Town	6	Kings Langley	5	(aet)
Round 2	Ampthill Town	1	Tring Athletic	4	
Round 2	Wembley	3	Brantham Athletic	4	(aet)
Round 2	Great Yarmouth Town	2	Hadleigh United	0	
Round 2	Erith Town	0	Phoenix Sports	3	
Round 2	Lingfield	5	Chessington & Hook United	1	
Round 2	Horndean	0	Ascot United	1	
Round 2	Hassocks	0	Ashford United	7	
Round 2	Hanworth Villa	1	Knaphill	0	
Round 2	Eastbourne United	1	Horley Town	3	
Round 2	Horsham YMCA	1	Erith & Belvedere	2	
Round 2	Abingdon United	4	Littlehampton Town	4	(aet)
Round 2	East Preston	0	Flackwell Heath	8	
Round 2	Westfield	1	Tunbridge Wells	5	
Round 2	Pagham	1	Colliers Wood United	2	
Round 2	United Services Portsmouth	1	AFC Portchester	3	
Round 2	Crawley Down Gatwick	1	Greenwich Borough	3	
Round 2	Newport (IW)	3	Loxwood	2	
Round 2	Alresford Town	3	Thame United	1	

Round 2	Odd Down	3	Hallen	2		
Round 2	Verwood Town	5	Plymouth Parkway	4		
Round 2	Folland Sports	2	AFC St. Austell	3		
Round 2	Buckland Athletic	2	Bristol Manor Farm	1		
Round 2	Chippenham Park	1	Bradford Town	2	(aet)	
Round 2	Blackfield & Langley	5	Bemerton Heath Harlequins	0		
Round 2	Melksham Town	2	Slimbridge	2	(aet)	
Round 2	Bodmin Town	5	St. Blazey	2		
Round 2	Highworth Town	3	Bridport	0		
Round 2	Shepton Mallet	1	Welton Rovers	0		
Replay	Littlehampton Town	7	Abingdon United	3		
Replay	Slimbridge	1	Melksham Town	4		
Round 3	Whitley Bay	1	Dunston UTS	2		
Round 3	1874 Northwich	0	Glossop North End	3		
Round 3	Shaw Lane Aquaforce	3	Shildon	2		
Round 3	Chadderton	2	Newcastle Benfield	1		
Round 3	Seaham Red Star	2	North Shields	4		
Round 3	St. Helens Town	2	Tadcaster Albion	4		
Round 3	Consett	3	Marske United	2		
Round 3	Worksop Town	2	Westfields	1		
Round 3	Thurnby Nirvana	2	Bromsgrove Sporting	1		
Round 3	Bolehall Swifts	0	Brocton	5		
Round 3	Mickleover Royals	0	AFC Mansfield	1		
Round 3	Wisbech Town	2	Walsall Wood	3		
Round 3	Deeping Rangers	1	Heanor Town	2	(aet)	
Round 3	Saffron Walden Town	1	AFC Dunstable	0		
Round 3	Hullbridge Sports	1	Great Yarmouth Town	0		
Round 3	St. Margaretsbury	0	Stanway Rovers	2		
Round 3	Peterborough Northern Star	2	Flackwell Heath	3		
Round 3	Tring Athletic	0	Norwich United	1		
Round 3	London Colney	0	Holbeach United	1		
Round 3	Brantham Athletic	1	Yaxley	3		
Round 3	Hanworth Villa	0	Erith & Belvedere	2		
Round 3	Alresford Town	1	Phoenix Sports	2		
Round 3	Horley Town	1	Greenwich Borough	3		
Round 3	AFC Portchester	0	Tunbridge Wells	1		
Round 3	Colliers Wood United	9	Lingfield	2		
Round 3	Ascot United	3	Newport (IW)	0		
Round 3	Littlehampton Town	3	Ashford United	3	(aet)	
Round 3	Melksham Town	3	Shepton Mallet	2		
Round 3	Blackfield & Langley	0	Highworth Town	1		
Round 3	AFC St. Austell	6	Verwood Town	1		
Round 3	Buckland Athletic	1	Bodmin Town	4		
Round 3	Bradford Town	4	Odd Down	3		
Replay	Ashford United	2	Littlehampton Town	1		
Round 4	Walsall Wood	1	Shaw Lane Aquaforce	1	(aet)	
Round 4	North Shields	4	Consett	1		
Round 4	Thurnby Nirvana	3	Holbeach United	4	(aet)	
Round 4	Chadderton	0	AFC Mansfield	5		
Round 4	Worksop Town	0	Glossop North End	1	(aet)	
Round 4	Heanor Town	0	Dunston UTS	1		
Round 4	Tadcaster Albion	3	Brocton	2		
Round 4	Bodmin Town	0	Phoenix Sports	2		
Round 4	Stanway Rovers	1	Saffron Walden Town	0		
Round 4	Ascot United	4	Colliers Wood United	2	(aet)	

Round 4	Bradford Town	3	Melksham Town	1	
Round 4	Ashford United	0	Norwich United	5	
Round 4	Greenwich Borough	2	AFC St. Austell	3	
Round 4	Flackwell Heath	3	Hullbridge Sports	0	
Round 4	Erith & Belvedere	1	Yaxley	0	
Round 4	Highworth Town	1	Tunbridge Wells	1	(aet)
Replay	Shaw Lane Aquaforce	4	Walsall Wood	1	
Replay	Tunbridge Wells	2	Highworth Town	2	(aet)
	Highworth Town won 4-2 on penalties				
Round 5	Bradford Town	0	Highworth Town	2	
Round 5	AFC St. Austell	2	Stanway Rovers	0	
Round 5	Ascot United	3	Norwich United	0	
Round 5	Shaw Lane Aquaforce	3	Flackwell Heath	2	
Round 5	Glossop North End	2	Dunston UTS	2	(aet)
Round 5	Holbeach United	2	Erith & Belvedere	3	(aet)
Round 5	North Shields	4	Phoenix Sport	1	
Round 5	AFC Mansfield	0	Tadcaster Albion	3	
Replay	Dunston UTS	1	Glossop North End	3	(aet)
Round 6	AFC St. Austell	3	Ascot United	2	
Round 6	Erith & Belvedere	0	North Shields	2	
Round 6	Shaw Lane Aquaforce	2	Glossop North End	2	(aet)
Round 6	Highworth Town	1	Tadcaster Albion	1	(aet)
Replay	Glossop North End	3	Shaw Lane Aquaforce	1	(aet)
Replay	Tadcaster Albion	0	Highworth Town	1	
Semi-finals					
1st leg	Highworth Town	0	North Shields	1	
1st leg	AFC St. Austell	0	Glossop North End	2	
2nd leg	North Shields	2	Highworth Town	0	
	North Shields won 3-0 on aggregate				
2nd leg	Glossop North End	0	AFC St. Austell	1	
	Glossop North End won 2-1 on aggregate				
FINAL	North Shields	2	Glossop North End	1	(aet)

Cup Statistics provided by:

www.soccerdata.com

National League Fixtures 2015/2016 Season	Aldershot Town	Altrincham	Barrow	Boreham Wood	Braintree Town	Bromley	Cheltenham Town	Chester	Dover Athletic	Eastleigh	Forest Green Rovers	Gateshead	Grimsby Town	Guiseley	FC Halifax Town	Kidderminster Harriers	Lincoln City	Macclesfield Town	Southport	Torquay United	Tranmere Rovers	Welling United	Woking	Wrexham
Aldershot Town		10/10	02/04	16/04	28/03	17/10	28/11	09/01	18/08	29/08	06/10	08/08	01/03	19/12	05/09	30/01	10/11	26/09	23/04	12/03	13/02	15/09	26/12	21/11
Altrincham	19/03		03/10	21/11	19/09	09/04	05/09	26/12	30/01	15/09	08/08	09/01	18/08	20/02	06/10	13/10	13/02	05/03	28/03	31/10	29/08	23/04	26/01	05/12
Barrow	19/09	12/03		05/12	20/02	19/03	06/02	06/10	08/08	05/09	27/02	26/12	10/11	18/08	28/03	26/09	15/09	09/04	29/08	14/11	09/01	17/10	28/11	30/04
Boreham Wood	13/10	26/09	05/03		26/12	15/09	09/01	14/11	28/03	23/01	18/08	31/10	05/09	23/04	08/08	06/02	24/11	19/03	09/04	20/02	28/11	10/10	29/08	19/09
Braintree Town	31/08	30/04	12/09	02/01		26/03	19/03	30/01	13/10	05/03	09/04	06/02	10/10	26/09	23/02	21/11	11/08	31/10	22/08	28/11	15/08	28/12	22/09	19/12
Bromley	30/04	14/11	10/10	10/11	18/08		13/10	26/09	29/08	26/12	28/03	05/09	05/12	12/03	06/02	22/09	02/04	12/09	09/01	16/04	23/01	01/03	20/02	08/08
Cheltenham Town	11/08	19/12	22/08	26/03	06/10	30/01		05/12	12/09	17/10	21/11	27/02	02/04	10/11	16/04	02/01	30/04	15/09	15/08	28/12	26/09	13/02	12/03	31/08
Chester	06/02	02/01	26/03	02/04	08/08	05/03	18/04		24/11	19/09	05/09	30/04	15/09	31/08	17/10	10/11	10/10	28/12	23/01	19/12	27/02	16/04	21/11	03/10
Dover Athletic	05/12	22/08	21/11	31/08	15/09	28/12	23/01	15/08		10/11	30/04	13/02	16/04	19/09	02/04	11/08	27/02	17/10	06/02	26/03	12/03	02/01	26/09	10/10
Eastleigh	28/12	16/04	13/02	11/08	03/10	02/01	01/03	12/03	22/09		13/10	12/09	21/11	02/04	31/10	19/12	15/08	22/08	28/11	31/08	23/04	26/03	27/02	30/01
Forest Green Rovers	26/03	28/11	15/08	19/12	23/01	31/08	22/09	31/10	14/11	20/02		26/09	05/03	10/10	23/04	28/12	22/08	30/01	12/09	02/01	17/10	11/08	16/04	02/04
Gateshead	20/02	17/10	02/01	15/08	16/04	23/04	10/10	28/11	03/10	16/02	12/03		30/01	28/12	21/11	22/08	31/08	26/03	10/11	02/04	11/08	19/09	19/12	15/09
Grimsby Town	12/09	23/01	11/08	13/02	12/03	15/08	31/10	23/04	19/12	09/04	03/10	06/10		02/01	13/10	28/11	28/12	31/08	27/02	22/08	19/09	14/11	06/02	26/03
Guiseley	22/08	11/08	24/11	17/10	27/02	28/11	09/04	28/03	19/03	14/11	09/01	29/08	26/12		15/09	15/08	03/10	06/10	22/09	30/04	06/02	31/10	12/09	05/03
FC Halifax Town	09/04	26/03	31/08	27/02	14/11	22/08	03/10	11/08	28/11	19/03	13/02	22/09	20/02	05/12		12/09	02/01	30/04	19/09	15/08	19/12	30/01	10/10	28/12
Kidderminster Harr.	14/11	02/04	16/04	06/10	05/09	27/02	26/12	20/02	23/04	09/01	29/08	05/12	08/08	23/01	12/03		19/09	13/02	17/10	15/09	28/03	03/10	31/10	18/08
Lincoln City	05/03	22/09	19/12	12/09	17/10	31/10	08/08	09/04	09/01	06/02	23/02	28/03	29/08	30/01	26/12	19/03		18/08	20/02	26/09	14/11	28/11	23/04	05/09
Macclesfield Town	23/01	10/11	22/09	03/10	02/04	21/11	23/04	29/08	20/02	05/12	19/09	13/10	28/03	16/04	09/01	10/10	12/03		11/08	06/02	26/12	15/08	05/09	27/02
Southport	31/10	31/08	28/12	30/01	13/02	19/12	14/11	13/10	05/09	08/08	05/12	18/08	26/09	26/03	05/03	30/04	16/04	23/02		10/10	15/09	12/03	02/04	02/01
Torquay United	03/10	27/02	23/04	22/09	09/01	19/09	29/08	13/02	06/10	28/03	26/12	23/01	17/10	05/09	16/02	05/03	21/11	08/08	19/03		09/04	05/12	18/08	10/11
Tranmere Rovers	22/09	28/12	13/10	22/08	05/12	03/10	20/02	12/09	31/10	10/10	19/03	05/03	30/04	21/11	18/08	31/08	26/03	02/01	09/02	30/01		02/04	08/08	16/04
Welling United	27/02	06/02	23/01	30/04	29/08	06/10	05/03	22/09	26/12	18/08	10/11	19/03	09/01	08/08	26/09	09/04	13/10	19/12	21/11	12/09	05/09		28/03	20/02
Woking	02/01	15/08	30/01	28/12	10/11	11/08	19/09	22/08	05/03	30/04	15/09	09/04	19/03	13/02	23/01	26/03	05/12	14/11	03/10	13/10	24/11	31/08		17/10
Wrexham	15/08	12/09	31/10	12/03	23/04	13/02	28/03	19/03	09/04	26/09	06/02	14/11	22/09	13/10	29/08	23/02	23/01	28/11	26/12	11/08	06/10	22/08	09/01	

Please note that the above fixtures may be subject to change.

National League North Fixtures 2015/2016 Season

	AFC Fylde	AFC Telford United	Alfreton Town	Boston United	Brackley Town	Bradford Park Avenue	Chorley	Corby Town	Curzon Ashton	FC United of Manchester	Gainsborough Trinity	Gloucester City	Harrogate Town	Hednesford Town	Lowestoft Town	North Ferriby United	Nuneaton Town	Solihull Moors	Stalybridge Celtic	Stockport County	Tamworth	Worcester City
AFC Fylde		03/10	27/02	05/03	14/11	26/03	02/01	26/01	28/12	15/09	15/08	13/02	23/04	11/08	22/08	09/04	19/03	19/12	31/10	31/08	12/09	23/01
AFC Telford United	30/01		31/10	20/02	31/08	23/01	05/03	19/03	11/08	09/02	22/08	28/12	12/09	02/01	19/12	19/09	14/11	09/04	17/10	15/08	26/03	23/04
Alfreton Town	07/11	01/03		21/11	15/08	19/12	23/01	20/02	22/08	19/03	31/08	26/03	09/04	12/09	11/08	24/10	30/01	28/12	03/10	23/04	02/01	15/09
Boston United	19/09	06/02	17/10		26/03	09/04	12/09	14/11	15/08	31/10	28/12	22/08	10/11	23/01	02/01	19/03	23/04	11/08	13/02	19/12	31/08	27/02
Brackley Town	02/04	28/03	09/01	18/08		12/03	16/04	26/12	07/11	16/01	17/10	05/12	08/08	19/09	15/09	05/09	13/02	30/01	21/11	20/02	30/04	29/08
Bradford Park Avenue	19/08	05/09	08/08	16/01	03/10		27/01	06/02	05/03	26/12	30/04	17/10	28/03	21/11	31/10	29/08	09/01	12/09	05/12	13/02	19/03	16/04
Chorley	26/12	30/04	05/09	12/03	31/10	14/11		09/01	19/03	18/08	09/04	16/01	29/08	17/10	27/02	05/12	08/08	03/10	28/03	15/09	30/01	13/02
Corby Town	17/10	07/11	02/04	16/09	02/01	22/08	15/08		19/12	09/04	23/01	12/08	21/11	26/03	28/12	05/03	27/02	31/08	23/04	30/01	13/02	19/09
Curzon Ashton	29/08	05/12	16/01	09/01	23/04	27/02	21/11	08/08		28/03	31/10	16/04	17/08	02/04	13/02	14/11	05/09	29/02	26/12	17/10	03/10	12/03
FC United of Man.	12/03	24/10	13/02	02/04	22/08	02/01	26/03	12/09	31/08		14/11	19/12	30/01	28/12	23/01	27/02	07/11	30/04	16/04	11/08	15/08	03/10
Gainsborough Trinity	09/01	16/01	28/03	29/08	09/02	30/01	24/10	05/09	06/02	23/04		02/04	05/12	07/11	16/04	26/12	12/03	20/02	18/08	03/10	15/09	08/08
Gloucester City	05/09	29/08	18/08	31/01	09/04	24/11	06/02	31/10	24/10	08/08	19/09		03/10	05/03	14/11	23/04	28/03	19/03	09/01	23/01	20/02	26/12
Harrogate Town	24/10	12/03	14/11	16/04	19/12	31/08	28/12	30/04	26/03	20/02	11/08	27/02		15/08	06/02	15/09	19/09	23/01	02/04	02/01	22/08	31/10
Hednesford Town	05/12	26/12	12/03	05/09	27/02	23/04	20/02	18/08	30/01	29/08	13/02	15/09	09/01		03/10	16/01	24/10	14/11	08/08	19/03	09/04	28/03
Lowestoft Town	16/01	08/08	05/12	26/12	05/03	20/02	19/09	29/08	09/04	05/09	19/03	30/04	17/10	23/02		28/03	18/08	07/11	30/01	21/11	24/10	09/01
North Ferriby United	21/11	16/04	30/04	07/11	23/01	28/12	11/08	03/10	20/02	17/10	02/01	12/09	13/02	22/08	31/08		24/11	15/08	12/03	26/03	19/12	02/04
Nuneaton Town	06/02	02/04	16/04	03/10	11/08	15/08	19/12	05/12	23/01	21/11	12/09	31/08	05/03	30/04	26/03	31/10		02/01	15/09	22/08	28/12	20/02
Solihull Moors	08/08	13/02	29/08	05/12	24/10	02/04	23/04	28/03	19/09	06/02	05/03	21/11	05/09	16/04	12/03	09/01	26/12		16/01	31/10	27/02	18/08
Stalybridge Celtic	20/02	27/02	05/03	30/04	19/03	11/08	31/08	24/10	02/01	19/09	26/03	15/08	07/11	19/12	12/09	06/02	09/04	22/08		28/12	23/01	14/11
Stockport County	28/03	09/01	19/09	08/08	12/09	24/10	07/11	16/04	30/04	05/12	27/02	12/03	26/12	06/02	02/04	18/08	16/01	24/11	29/08		14/11	05/09
Tamworth	16/04	18/08	26/12	28/03	06/02	19/09	02/04	12/03	16/02	09/01	21/11	07/11	16/01	31/10	23/04	08/08	29/08	17/10	05/09	05/03		05/12
Worcester City	30/04	21/11	06/02	24/10	28/12	07/11	22/08	16/01	12/09	05/03	19/12	02/01	19/03	31/08	15/08	30/01	18/10	26/03	23/02	09/04	11/08	

Please note that the above fixtures may be subject to change.

National League South Fixtures 2015/2016 Season	Basingstoke Town	Bath City	Bishop's Stortford	Chelmsford City	Concord Rangers	Dartford	Eastbourne Borough	Ebbsfleet United	Gosport Borough	Havant & Waterlooville	Hayes & Yeading United	Hemel Hempstead Town	Maidenhead United	Maidstone United	Margate	Oxford City	St. Albans City	Sutton United	Truro City	Wealdstone	Weston-super-Mare	Whitehawk
Basingstoke Town		11/08	15/08	17/10	02/04	07/11	12/09	30/01	31/08	12/03	28/12	16/01	20/02	21/11	22/08	26/03	19/12	02/01	23/04	19/09	09/04	27/10
Bath City	03/10		19/03	31/10	23/01	05/09	16/04	12/03	01/03	29/08	05/12	12/09	18/08	09/01	30/04	14/11	20/02	17/10	26/12	08/08	28/03	06/02
Bishop's Stortford	05/12	07/11		18/08	29/08	24/10	12/03	23/04	23/01	08/08	13/02	02/02	03/10	20/02	16/04	02/04	26/12	14/11	27/02	28/03	05/09	09/01
Chelmsford City	30/04	02/04	22/02		14/09	26/12	21/11	24/10	16/04	05/09	15/08	10/08	12/03	28/03	20/02	03/10	29/08	30/01	07/11	19/12	09/01	23/01
Concord Rangers	14/11	09/04	28/12	26/03		18/08	06/02	02/01	20/02	23/04	17/10	22/08	24/11	31/10	31/08	12/09	19/03	05/12	16/01	05/03	08/08	19/09
Dartford	16/04	16/01	26/03	02/01	27/02		11/08	31/08	22/08	05/12	31/10	17/10	02/04	14/11	28/12	23/04	06/02	15/08	19/09	26/01	12/09	12/03
Eastbourne Borough	09/01	30/01	17/10	19/03	03/10	20/02		14/11	23/04	28/03	05/03	09/04	08/08	29/08	15/09	05/12	18/08	31/10	05/09	23/01	13/02	26/12
Ebbsfleet United	08/08	19/12	21/11	09/04	26/12	28/03	30/04		05/03	06/02	27/02	19/03	05/09	03/10	23/01	07/11	16/02	15/09	09/01	31/10	18/08	29/08
Gosport Borough	28/03	15/09	09/04	05/12	12/03	30/01	16/01	17/10		26/12	30/04	31/10	06/02	05/09	19/09	27/02	08/08	19/03	29/08	09/01	14/11	18/08
Havant & Waterloo.	23/01	28/12	16/01	13/02	19/12	19/03	31/08	19/09	02/01		26/03	05/03	14/11	27/02	15/08	22/08	31/10	11/08	09/04	17/10	30/04	15/09
Hayes & Yeading Utd	29/08	23/04	12/09	14/11	16/04	09/01	24/10	02/04	03/10	18/08		23/01	28/03	19/12	06/02	20/02	12/03	01/03	22/11	05/09	26/12	08/08
Hemel Hempstead T.	05/09	27/02	19/09	06/02	24/10	08/08	07/11	05/12	02/04	09/01	15/09		29/08	18/08	21/11	16/04	28/03	20/02	12/03	26/12	30/01	30/04
Maidenhead United	31/10	26/03	11/08	19/09	30/04	21/11	27/02	16/01	15/08	30/01	31/08	28/12		15/09	05/03	02/01	09/04	22/08	19/03	13/02	17/10	05/12
Maidstone United	05/03	19/09	30/04	31/08	30/01	09/04	28/12	11/08	13/02	12/09	22/08	26/03	24/10		02/01	15/08	17/10	16/01	05/12	17/11	19/03	07/11
Margate	13/02	24/10	30/01	16/01	28/03	29/08	23/02	12/09	19/12	07/11	19/03	23/04	09/01	26/12		12/03	05/09	09/04	08/08	18/08	03/10	14/11
Oxford City	18/08	05/03	31/10	08/08	09/01	15/09	19/09	13/02	21/11	10/11	09/04	19/12	26/12	06/02	17/10		23/01	30/04	28/03	19/03	29/08	05/09
St. Albans City	14/09	22/08	02/01	28/12	13/02	30/04	26/03	15/08	24/10	16/04	19/09	31/08	07/11	02/04	05/12	10/08		05/03	30/01	14/11	16/01	27/02
Sutton United	26/12	13/02	06/02	23/04	05/09	23/01	02/04	16/04	12/09	21/11	07/11	03/10	19/12	08/08	27/02	24/10	09/01		17/08	29/08	12/03	28/03
Truro City	24/10	02/01	22/08	05/03	15/08	13/02	19/12	20/02	28/12	03/10	11/08	14/11	23/01	16/04	31/10	31/08	12/09	26/03		30/04	01/03	02/04
Wealdstone	27/02	21/11	31/08	12/09	10/08	03/10	15/08	22/08	07/11	02/04	30/01	02/01	16/04	12/03	26/03	16/01	23/04	28/12	06/02		05/12	24/10
Weston-super-Mare	06/02	31/08	19/12	27/02	07/11	05/03	22/08	26/03	11/08	24/10	02/01	15/08	23/04	23/01	02/04	28/12	21/11	19/09	15/09	20/02		16/04
Whitehawk	19/03	15/08	05/03	22/08	21/11	19/12	02/01	28/12	26/03	20/02	16/01	13/02	12/09	23/04	11/08	30/01	03/10	31/08	17/10	09/04	31/10	

Please note that the above fixtures may be subject to change.

NON-LEAGUE CLUB DIRECTORY 2016

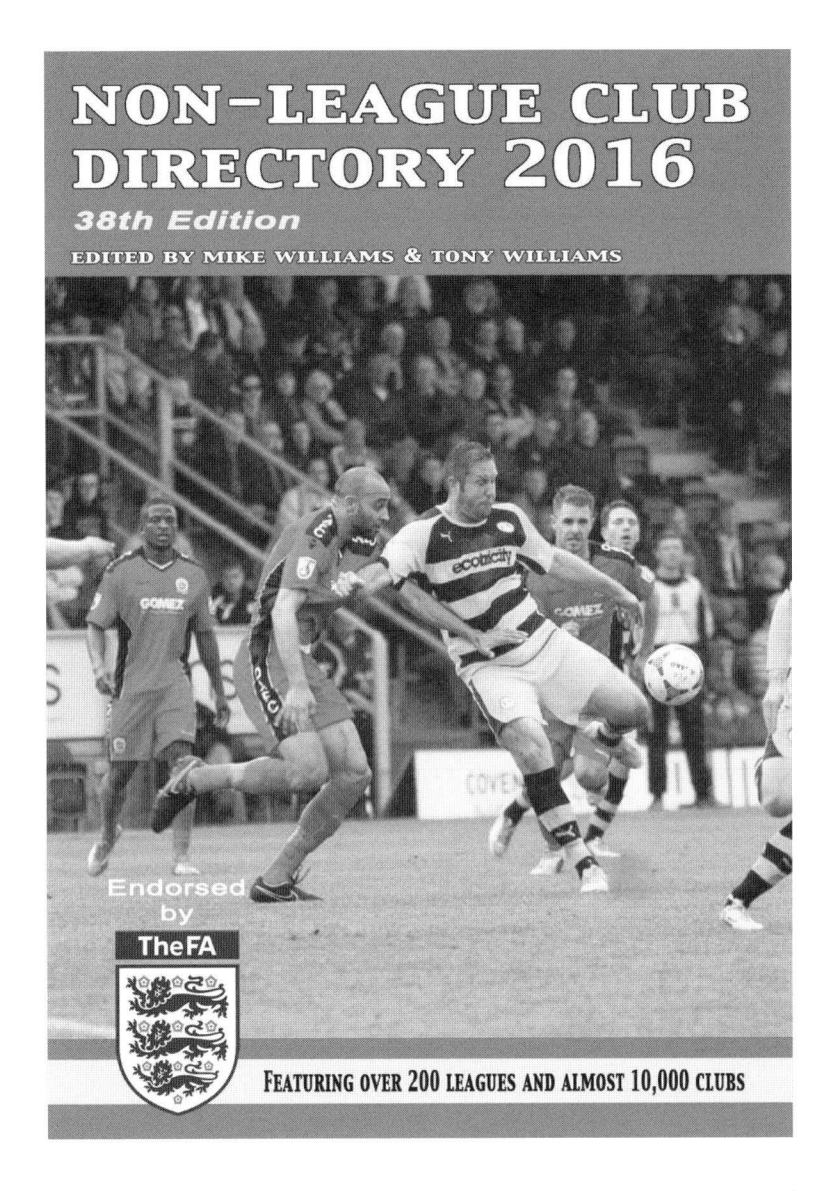

38th Edition

EDITED BY MIKE WILLIAMS & TONY WILLIAMS

Endorsed by The FA

FEATURING OVER 200 LEAGUES AND ALMOST 10,000 CLUBS

Now in its 38th year of publication, The Directory has developed into a comprehensive record of competitions within the non-league game and gives this level of football the publicity and prestige it deserves.

The Football Association has encouraged the development of the publication since its introduction as a small pocket book in 1978 and all their competitions such as The Cup, Trophy and Vase plus their Youth and Women's cups are featured.

Individual club pages highlight the top twelve divisions with club details, records and statistics plus senior players are featured in team photographs and within many action shots from league and cup football.

Major competitions within the nation's pyramid of domestic leagues are featured from levels 1-7 with many leagues outside of the top seven steps also featured.

The Supporters' Guides Series

This top-selling series has been published since 1982 and the new 2016 editions contain the 2014/2015 Season's results and tables, Directions, Photographs, Telephone numbers, Parking information, Admission details, Disabled information and much more.

THE SUPPORTERS' GUIDE TO PREMIER & FOOTBALL LEAGUE CLUBS 2016

This 32nd edition covers all 92 Premiership and Football League clubs. *Price £9.99*

NON-LEAGUE SUPPORTERS' GUIDE AND YEARBOOK 2016

This 24th edition covers all 68 clubs in Step 1 & Step 2 of Non-League football – the Vanarama National League, National League North and National League South. *Price £9.99*

SCOTTISH FOOTBALL SUPPORTERS' GUIDE AND YEARBOOK 2016

The 23rd edition featuring all Scottish Professional Football League, Highland League and Lowland League clubs. *Price £9.99*

THE SUPPORTERS' GUIDE TO WELSH FOOTBALL 2011

The 12th edition covers the 112+ clubs which make up the top 3 tiers of Welsh Football. *Price £8.99*

RYMAN FOOTBALL LEAGUE SUPPORTERS' GUIDE AND YEARBOOK 2011

The 1st edition features the 66 clubs which made up the 3 divisions of the Isthmian League during the 2010/11 season. *Price £6.99*

ZAMARETTO SOUTHERN FOOTBALL LEAGUE SUPPORTERS' GUIDE AND YEARBOOK 2011

This 1st edition features the 66 clubs which made up the 3 divisions of the Southern League during the 2010/11 season. *Price £6.99*

These books are available UK & Surface post free from –

Soccer Books Limited (Dept. SBL)
72 St. Peter's Avenue
Cleethorpes, DN35 8HU
United Kingdom